# THE FORGOTTEN LANGUAGE

# THE FORGOTTEN LANGUAGE

*Contemporary Poets and Nature*

**EDITED BY CHRISTOPHER MERRILL**

PEREGRINE SMITH BOOKS
SALT LAKE CITY

95 94     8 7 6 5 4

Preface and introduction copyright © 1991 by Christopher Merrill.
All rights reserved.
Copyrights for individual poems are noted on pages 171 - 176.
Cover Art: *The Blackbird Brings the Message,*
acrylic on canvas by Bonnie Sucec

Design by Kathleen Timmerman
Manufactured in the United States of America

**Library of Congress Cataloging-in-Publication Data**
The Forgotten language: contemporary poets and nature / edited by
    Christopher Merrill.
        p.      cm.
    ISBN 0-87905-376-3
    1. Nature – Poetry.  2. American poetry – 20th century.
I. Merrill, Christopher.
PS595.N22F67    1991
811'.508036 – dc20                                        90-49745
                                                              CIP

I want to tell what the forests
were like

I will have to speak
in a forgotten language

—W. S. Merwin

5/31/2001
La Jolla

Here. The sky is full of green.

Cannot look up, for

the yellow fills ~~that is~~

for that direction only.

spring—~~[illegible]~~ ~~chilly~~ & sl[illegible]—

[illegible] [illegible] [illegible] blowing [illegible]—

~~[illegible]~~ [illegible] of [illegible] [illegible], ([illegible])

& heavy [illegible] for [illegible] [illegible]

[illegible] [illegible] [illegible]—which I look up,

there [illegible] [illegible] [illegible] [illegible] :

[illegible] [illegible], [illegible] [illegible] [illegible]

[illegible] & spit at.

and there, as always, I must [illegible]—

Boredom [illegible] [illegible] of obligation

[illegible] [illegible] [illegible] [illegible].

[illegible] — in all this [illegible]

([illegible] that [illegible] [illegible] [illegible] [illegible] —)

the [illegible] is [illegible] [illegible] [illegible]

by streams of yellow [illegible] & [illegible] [illegible]—

[illegible] [illegible] [illegible] [illegible] — [illegible].

[illegible]! — [illegible] [illegible] & [illegible] [illegible]—

But [illegible] [illegible] [illegible] [illegible] [illegible]—

The [illegible] of [illegible] [illegible] [illegible] not [illegible]

till we look up.

[illegible] [illegible] [illegible] [illegible] [illegible]!! [illegible] [illegible] [illegible]!! [illegible]?

for Brewster Ghiselin

*"All the field, savored in the one wild dewberry."*

# BOOKSTAR
STORE # 1841 TUSTIN, CA 714-731-2302

REG#01      BOOKSELLER#013
RECEIPT#   39922  05/04/97   6:31 PM


# CUSTOMER COPY

S 0879053763     FORGOTTEN LANG
                    1 @ 15.95    15.95

SUBTOTAL                          15.95
SALES TAX - 7.75%                  1.24
TOTAL                             17.19
VISA PAYMENT                      17.19
ACCOUNT# 4209730000180516   EXP 1098
AUTHORIZATION# 004373       CLERK  13

     THANKS FOR SHOPPING AT BOOKSTAR

# CONTENTS

# PREFACE

THE SANGRE DE CRISTO Mountains in Northern New Mexico are a popular stopping place on the leaf-watching circuit. Here in the Rockies autumn's frosts turn one of the largest aspen stands in the continental United States a brilliant shade of gold. The "quakies," as the majestic trees overlooking Santa Fe are called, are nearing the end of their hundred-year-long life cycle, and in September we witness the passing not just of a season but of an era. For if nature is allowed to run its course, in the next ten years or so the aspens will start dying off, giving way to the fir and spruce seedlings growing now in their shadows. In time a climax forest again may blanket the steeps of these rugged mountains.

*If* nature is allowed to run its course.

Tourism is big business in Santa Fe: the town fathers are reluctant to give up the crowds of leaf-watchers who fill the hotels and restaurants, swelling the city's coffers. Thus periodically a local politician proposes to replant the entire aspen stand—thousands of acres of aspens! The Forest Service, one wing of which is committed to "forest management for viewing purposes," would burn down all the trees; a new generation of aspens would fill the disturbed area, stopping nature's clock. What is now transition forest would remain in transition. Each fall for the next century sheets of gold would cover the Sangre de Cristoes.

It is difficult to tell if this plan, which has backers in both the business community and the Forest Service, is more dangerous than ridiculous. How would such a "controlled" fire be contained if, for example, the wind picked up? What would happen to the birds and animals in the burn area? And the leafwatchers—where would they go while the young aspens matured? These were just a few of the questions Gibbs and Cathy Smith, publishers of Peregrine Smith Books, raised one September afternoon, as we hiked up Aspen Vista, a well-worn trail near my home in Santa Fe.

Under the spell of the turning leaves we came up with a plan of our own—an anthology of contemporary poets and nature, designed in part to counter the kind of thinking that leads men to believe they can burn down an aspen stand with impunity. A little over a hundred years ago Gerard Manley Hopkins, dejected by the felling of another aspen grove, wrote of nature: "even where we mean / To mend her we end her, / When we hew or delve: / After-comers cannot guess the beauty been." What we proposed was to put together a book of poems for a readership on the verge of becoming "after-comers" to the beauty of the whole planet.

My first debt of gratitude, then, is to Gibbs and Cathy, who encouraged me to do this book. Thanks also to James and Denise Thomas for their invaluable advice on editorial matters; to Agha Shahid Ali, who read and critiqued the introduction; and to the crew at Peregrine Smith—Madge Baird, Heather Bennett, and Steve Chapman—who provided their usual expertise and enthusiasm. A number of poets offered helpful suggestions, including Brewster Ghiselin, William Heyen, Leslie Norris, and David St. John. Alexanna Padilla and Ann Shields handled the secretarial chores. Mary Van Ness typed the manuscript in what can only be termed heroic fashion. And my wife, Lisa, helped in ways too numerous to mention. Finally, I want to thank the poets who made their work available to me: without them *The Forgotten Language* would still be in the planning stages.

Christopher Merrill
Santa Fe, New Mexico

# INTRODUCTION

*"When we see land as a community to which we belong,
we may begin to use it with love and respect."*
*—Aldo Leopold*

"THERE IS A SPIRIT in the woods," Wordsworth declared at the end of "Nutting," his visionary poem of 1798. Echoed in one form or another by countless writers since the dawning of the modern age, his notion of immanence continues to fuel the debate over man's place in the natural order. What should our relationship to nature be? is a question no one in good conscience today can ignore. And poets offer some of the most interesting, if modest, answers. Interesting not only for the descriptive beauty their poems may possess, but also for the variety and complexity of their responses; modest in the sense that a nature poem is at best a partial account of a subject too large for anyone to grasp. Yet these "partial accounts" form an impressive body of literature, a poetic tradition rich enough to make this anthology possible—and perhaps even necessary. For what these poems suggest in their various ways is the need to respect the earth, which has suffered so much at our hands. Whether we believe in immanence or not, our survival as a species will depend on our adopting a different attitude toward nature—an attitude poets can help articulate.

Consider, for example, Wordsworth's recollection in "Nutting" of a vision granted him in childhood: his innocent journey into the woods to gather hazel nuts takes on philosophical significance as soon as he inexplicably yanks down the branch of a tree. Rising to his feet, "[e]xulting, rich beyond the wealth of kings," the boy discovers to his chagrin that he has desecrated a sacred place and thus betrayed the whole of nature. He has, in fact, lost his innocence; and his recognition of that loss ushers in the revelation of immanence he will one day pass on to others. Chastened, cast out of another Garden of Eden, the boy grows up to be the poet who will learn, as he writes in "Lines Composed a Few Miles Above Tintern Abbey," that nature is the "anchor of [his] purest thoughts, the nurse, / The guide, the guardian of [his] heart, and soul / Of all [his] moral being." He must never dishonor it again.

As the twentieth century draws to a close, we find ourselves in much the same position Wordsworth was in once he realized he had turned that hazel grove into a "mutilated bower." Since his time the evidence of our desecration of nature has grown overwhelming: whole ecosystems have vanished under our stewardship, thousands of species of plants and animals have become extinct, and traces of industrial pollution have been detected everywhere—even under Antarctica's ice shelf. In 1988, to take only the most recent (and glaring) set of statistics, the United States discharged into the air, earth, and water 22 *billion* pounds of toxic wastes. No one can gauge what the final consequences of our folly will be, but we have witnessed enough environmental disasters to know we are in serious trouble. Love Canal, Bhopal, Chernobyl—these are the names of places a poet might memorialize, writing them "out in a verse," as Yeats did in 1916 for the Irish martyrs of the Easter Rebellion.

Today the earth itself has been martyred, in the name of progress. Oil spills; acid rain; dying forests and lakes in the Northern Hemisphere; the destruction of tropical rain forests; the depletion of the ozone layer; the Greenhouse Effect; the poisoning of our food chain; —all attest to our collective arrogance toward nature. Like the ancient Greek playwrights who dramatized the hubris of certain characters in order to purge their audiences of arrogance, poets in the 1990s have little choice but to confront the evidence of our own hubris. And this they have done in exemplary fashion, protesting on the one hand our abuses of the earth and praising on the other what Pliny called the "least things" of nature.

Wendell Berry believes contemporary nature poetry is "a secular pilgrimage," a way of writing that "seeks the world of the creation" in a worshipful manner. Avoiding conventional religious doctrines, it nevertheless retains a sacred character: a poet's trek into the wild may resemble a religious quest, and a poem resulting from such a quest can inspire in its readers reverence for the natural world, humility and awe in the face of the creation—feelings often associated with the experience of the divine. Wordsworth, of course, felt this again and again on his rambles through the English countryside, and at first glance "a secular pilgrimage" might seem to be simply another version of the Romantic idea of the search for the sublime. But there is a difference now: "Because of the wounds to nature in our time," as John Elder writes in his excellent study of poets and nature, *Imagining the Earth,* "we must learn, for the first time or not at all, to become true servants of the earth."

What does it mean to "serve" the earth? For poets such service begins with the language itself. "The writer's morality does not lie in the subjects he deals with or the arguments he sets forth," the Mexican poet and critic Octavio Paz notes, "but in his behavior toward the language." Those who serve the language, recognizing it has a life of its own, a life they have an artistic obligation to honor, may be particularly well-suited to serve a vision of the natural world. Language, like nature, is an order larger than any individual; poets surrender to that order, hoping to discover in the process meanings they were not aware of when they sat down to write. The same may hold for their experience of the wild. As Wendell Berry explains:

> The nature poets of our time characteristically approach their subject with an openness of spirit and imagination, allowing the meaning and the movement of the poem to suggest themselves out of the facts. Their art has an implicit and essential humility, a reluctance to impose on things as they are, a willingness to relate to the world as student and servant, a wish to be included in the natural order rather than to "conquer nature," a wish to discover the natural form rather than to create new forms that would be exclusively human. To create is to involve oneself as fully, as consciously and imaginatively, as possible in the creation, to be immersed in the world.

Immersion in the world requires poets to keep their eyes open. Observation is the key to any fieldwork, including the task of gathering notes for a poem. Emerson reminds us that "there is no fact in nature which does not carry the whole sense of nature"; it is from the observation of such facts that poets, ever alert to the importance of concrete details, begin some of their finest work. Howard Nemerov has said a poem is "an act of attention," and each of the poems in this anthology asks its readers to pay attention to what they may be too busy to notice—a hedgeapple, sparrows, the way "the blueberry will turn ten acres red." Indeed, these "acts of attention" work against the accelerating pace of our society, constituting a subversive movement of sorts, counseling patience over and against the constant pressure to do more and more: "every day do something / that won't compute," Wendell Berry advises.

There is, then, a political component embedded in the tradition of nature poetry. Contrary to Terrence Des Pres' assertion that in recent years a number of American poets have abdicated their political responsibilities, refusing to engage the nuclear question while writing about nature, I would suggest their meditations on the workings of the natural world may be every bit as *engagé* as poems decrying the military-industrial complex. We are acutely aware of the nuclear threat; what we seem to overlook is the very real possibility that we will poison ourselves before any missiles are fired; hence the need for poems attentive to the ecological fate of the earth. Stanley Kunitz maintains "that to be a poet at all in twentieth-century America is to commit a political act." We should not underestimate the political ramifications of anyone's decision to be a poet in our day, including those who choose to write about nature.

A. R. Ammons, for one, has devoted considerable energy to exploring nature's intricacies. Admonishing readers "to be quiet in the hands of the marvelous," he himself finds examples of the marvelous everywhere—in a jay lighting on the branch of a tree, in the spider that "sizzles / in winter grasses," in gulches, mountains, maples. Like Thoreau, he is adept at the *art* of walking; much of his work is the record of his saunterings through nature. "Corsons Inlet," his famous poem set by the ocean, charts a journey over the dunes taken "in the spirit of undying adventure" Thoreau applauded. Here he discovers meaning in his attempts "to fasten into order enlarging grasps of disorder"; although each step brings him fresh news of his surroundings, it also reinforces his belief that "there is no finality of vision."

Yet his is a visionary poetry, which offers us scores of ways to apprehend the world. Convinced his task is to be a medium for whatever may bubble up out of the "black wells of possibility," Ammons writes that he is,

> not so much looking for the shape
> as being available
> to any shape that may be
> summoning itself
> through me
> from the self not mine but ours.

And that collective self is firmly grounded in the natural world.

David Wagoner's poetry reveals a similar openness of spirit. Landscapes, he has said, will blossom into poems for him, if he keeps his eyes and ears open. Sinking into nature, according to John Gardner, is how this poet finds "what is there, really there, and common with himself"—an imaginative and educational strategy with a moral imperative: "If what a tree or a bush does is lost on you," he warns, "You are surely lost." Indeed, his work fairly teems with characters who lose themselves in natural settings only to discover that within the confines of the larger universe they are very much at home. And this pantheistic version of Christ's injunction that "he who loses his life for my sake will find it" may have some bearing on Wagoner's writing methods; for he claims to generate poems by abandoning himself to the language, writing blindly in every direction until he uncovers the seeds of a poem, the images and ideas he can shape into a first draft. As poet and naturalist alike, he gives himself over to the whole range of language and experience.

His way of writing may remind us of the Surrealist experiments of the 1920s. The practice of automatic writing—writing in the absence of conscious control to express what André Breton called "the real functioning of thought"—is in certain respects akin to the search for the wild: the Surrealists' automatic texts and naturalists' journals share the same sense of exploration. Of course, the Surrealists were interested primarily in charting the hitherto unmapped regions of the unconscience, which is a far cry from, say, backpacking into the Brooks Range in Alaska. But their imaginative journeys—pilgrimages, if you will —resulted in profound discoveries, too: "Poetry is made in a forest," Breton wrote.

In *Imagining the Earth* John Elder equates wilderness areas with poetry—"[i]n both cases human reason draws and defends a boundary beyond which its own dominance will not be allowed." Such an idea, I would argue, might not be possible without the Surrealists' example: inspired in part by the proclamations and manifestoes published by Breton and his friends, for the last fifty years poets everywhere have written against the excesses of reason. In like manner, the poets in this anthology are working toward a more balanced vision of the world; although none is perhaps a Surrealist, few would deny they share with those antic Frenchmen the impulse to ride what Octavio Paz calls "the wave of the language."

The poems of W. S. Merwin often incorporate elements of Surrealism—the quest for the dark and primitive, disparate images, juxtaposition of different levels of discourse, free formal structures—and he joins the Surrealists in their commitment to political action. Merwin's activism frequently takes the form of writing on behalf of nature. In "Notes for a Preface" he explains why:

> among my peculiar failings is an inability to believe that the experience of being human, that gave rise to the arts in the first place, can continue to be nourished in a world contrived and populated by nothing but humans. No doubt such a situation is biologically impossible, but it is economically desirable, and we exist in an era dedicated to the myth that the biology of the planet, as well as anything else that may be, can be forced to adapt infinitely to the appetites of one species, organized and deified under the name of economics.

Thus it is not surprising to encounter a streak of anger in his work. To a gray whale "we are sending . . . to The End / That great god" he says: "Tell him / That it is we who are important." Nor should we be startled to learn that in recent poems his level of stridency has increased: as the plight of the earth grows more dire, the rancor of certain poets will rise. In the middle of the last century Thoreau described the New World as a volume with pages missing, pages of natural history destroyed since the settling of America. Merwin's lamentations have an altogether different tone, informed by his sense of urgency:

> I want to tell what the forests
> were like
>
> I will have to speak
> in a forgotten language

But as he has illustrated in several fine poems, praise is also an effective means of speaking in that forgotten language. The desire to praise is a constant in the history of nature poetry; in this century that tradition has taken on a new particularity. In the work of Stanley Kunitz, Margaret Atwood, Nancy Willard, Thomas McGrath, and a host of others it is not uncommon to read paeans to specific plants and animals; contemporary poets tap hidden reserves of psychic energy by turning their attention to the nonhuman. As D. H. Lawrence showed in *Birds, Beasts and Flowers,* arguably his strongest collection of poems, those who train their eyes on a snake, a fig tree, goats, etc., may produce their best work. "At my touch / the wild braid of creation / trembles," Kunitz writes in one poem. Elsewhere he makes plain the importance of participating in nature:

> The first step toward salvation was the recognition of the narrowness of my world of sympathies. My affections had to flow outward and circulate through the natural order of things. Only then did I understand that in the great chain of being, death has its own beauty and magnificence.

The question of our place in the great chain of being is equally central to Galway Kinnell. "The nonhuman *is* the 'basic context' of human existence," he has said. And in poems like "The Bear," which has been anthologized enough to warrant its exclusion here, or "The Porcupine" he summons animal spirits to his side, affirming his belief that "the mystery of the world isn't apprehended only by surrealist poems." In America, he once remarked,

> we have a rich tradition of evoking physical things, of giving the physical world actual presence. Our language has more physical verbs and more physical adjectives in it than most, and so has a peculiar capacity to bring into presence the creatures and things that the world is made up of. If the things and creatures that live on earth don't possess mystery, then there isn't any. To touch this mystery requires, I think, love of the things and creatures that surround us: the capacity to go out to them so that they enter us, so that they are transformed within us, and so that our own inner life finds expression through them.

Kinnell, James Dickey, Denise Levertov, Brewster Ghiselin, Sandra McPherson—these are some of the poets who conjure up the physical universe, celebrating the mystery inherent in nature. Like Williams and Rilke, Ponge and Neruda, they describe the things of the earth with such love and care that in their poems flowers, animals, winds and seas assume lives of their own. In "Song of Myself" Whitman announced: "I think I could turn and live awhile with the animals . . . they are so placid and self-contained, / I stand and look at them sometimes half the day long." Poets still heed his words, enlarging their sympathies by evoking the physical world, including its animals, no one of which "is demented with the mania of owning things," according to Whitman.

Whitman also wrote: "The known universe has one complete lover and that is the greatest poet." Who is that lover, that greatest poet? Perhaps it is poetry itself—the collected works of all the poets, living and dead, in every language. Certainly it numbers among its ranks those who glean facts and ideas from their fellow explorers in the natural sciences. Pattiann Rogers, for example, brings to her poetry the added dimension of extensive training as a zoologist. "What is it I don't know of myself / From never having seen a crimson chat at its feeding? / Or the dunnart carrying its young?" she wonders, knowing in advance her question is at once unanswerable and important. For it is the poet's fate to ask questions, which correspond to our deepest longings—and which may yet never be answered, if only because the poet, like the lover of the universe, is as interested in the unknown as in the known. Hence the difficulty of posing even the most elementary questions, to say nothing of the complicated ones poets routinely ask: Why are we here? What shall we do? Where do we fit in the natural order?

Such questions, it should be obvious, will assume many forms, reflecting the temperamental differences among various poets. Richard Wilbur, who feels "that the universe is full of glorious energy, that the energy tends to take pattern and shape, and that the ultimate character of things is comely and good," frames his questions in traditional forms—a choice favored by poets like Anthony Hecht, Richard Kenney, Leslie Norris, and Robert Pack. Believing there is order in the universe, they are not afraid to celebrate that order in ways it has been fashionable for some time in American poetry to disparage; their use of meter and rhyme, they might argue, is a function of nature's glory. As Wendy Salinger has pointed out: "Rhyme, which in its purest state is repetition, is the affinity of thing for thing (in the universe). The true 'rhymer' has a vision which says: 'only connect.'"

By the same token, Denise Levertov believes "there is a form in all things (and in our experience) which the poet can discover and reveal." Determined not to impose conventional forms on her material, she writes what she calls "organic verse," a partial definition of which "might be that it is a method of apperception,

> that is, of recognizing what we perceive, and is based on an intuition of an order, a form beyond forms, in which forms partake, and of which man's creative works are analogies, resemblances, natural allegories. Such poetry is exploratory.

Most poetry, of course, is exploratory; the sense of discovery is common to poets from all schools, traditional and otherwise. What sets Levertov apart—and unites her with Ezra Pound, among others—is her idea that in organic verse "the metric movement, the measure, is the direct expression of the movement of perception."

Many share her belief that the poet's obligation is, as Emerson suggested, to "[a]sk the fact for the form." From Whitman and Lawrence down to the present poets have invented nonce forms to capture ideas and images that might not fit into more traditional forms. "O taste and see," Levertov writes, encouraging us to revel in the life of the planet and thus heal the split between the nonhuman and human realms of existence. That her encouragement dispenses with regular metrics and rhyme does not diminish its power; the true test of a poem lies beyond formal and technical considerations even as it acknowledges the importance of such criteria. Has the poet established what Emerson recommended in "Nature," "an original relation with the universe?" That is what we must ask of our writers.

And there are scores of talented poets in this country establishing "original relations" with the universe. Just as America itself is distinguished by the diversity of its landscapes, so its nature poetry is marked by formal variety and a wealth of subject matter. Indeed, it was this diversity that convinced me to include in this anthology as many good poets as possible, rather than confine myself to a few of the very best. A selection of this kind will necessarily be limited by both editorial taste and page constraints, and I regret the number of excellent poems I had to exclude. In truth, once I began looking into this body of literature, I realized almost every first-rate poet in America has written first-rate nature poems. This anthology, then, is a partial (in all senses of the word) account of nature poetry; three hundred more pages might not cover the subject. Readers who explore further into this central tradition will not be disappointed.

"In Wildness is the preservation of the World," Thoreau wrote, a line which has become a cornerstone of the environmental movement. Each of the poems here is a plea on behalf of the wild—in the natural world and in poetry itself. Poets turn to nature for inspiration, images, and ideas, facts that correspond to their internal landscapes and needs, occasions to dream and meditate. And we turn to their poems for the same reasons, hoping to restore ourselves momentarily to the world outside our windows. If our poets must speak in what amounts to a forgotten language, that should only encourage us to preserve what is left of that language, that book of nature we persist in trying to read. How else will we honor the spirits still abroad in the woods?

# *Lucile Adler*

∎

## Shiprock

Where begging hands arch the hot aisles
And the desert prays crudely, no angel faces
Part the burning clouds, no guild of lovers
Carves the parapets with bloom;
Only sun thunders down and the loud
Wings of a bird assault the heat-cowled
Presence of the Stone

∎

We who made lenses of the burning sands,
Who see with our making hands, failed
Tests of vision, worship's tool,
By forcing nature's holy will
Into the glass our reason fused—
Now lightnings shatter seeds of rock,
Roots explode in booming light, and
Dreams we built crash to their knees.

∎

Who formed this Carcassonne of Stone
Where sun astounds and haloes burn
Over the last unyielding spires;
Where cold as granite angels' eyes
Our eyes once charged the potent aisles?
We kneel, and with the desert pray
For wings and clarity to bloom,
For the stone Presence to persist—

Our hands gone blind with wonder
Whose wonder broke Creation's fist.

# SQUIRREL

now let us celebrate the day
like any other day when the white
(almost white in the sun) squirrel
posed on the sharp roof ledge
above wood corbels carved long ago

stood on hind legs, thin claw hands
held out in benediction or malediction,
we couldn't tell which, over the white heat
of a drought day like any other
when the throats of mourning doves
dried in the sun by noon, the flowers
shook and looked white, there were rumors
of riots or rain that refused to come,
asbestos was lodged in the lung, and fat
granaries exploded; a day when plague
announced itself again in a dead coyote
furring the naked ground, and butterflies,
dark eyelets in their open wings, worked
drying clover at the desert's edge—

celebrate the squirrel on the roof
stock still and odd in the white light

potent with blessings or danger,
we don't know which, fixed there over
warning signs we still can't read, carved
black shadows clawing the old corbels.

# The Fox and the Flood

O quiet quiet as the fox through the bush
without leaves watches April rain and a house
slide quiet down the white and watchful dawn

the arroyo runs with news, skies betray and run
April into May over the fox's eye, and the bare
bush pulls at its root to outrun O quietly

catastrophe so common now even the hidden fox
senses something wrong, a season running away
and certainty awash—the fox hunts us or will,

bristling dry from the chilly brush, old burnished
fox aware of sly rumor air spreads freely, prowls
the flooded quiet where tyrants and rebels rise

and the carved white cornice falling, cries
take me swiftly down, twined with roots of bay
to the running familiar clay but quiet quietly—

through the blind rush sucking what used to be
fair destroyed and light leaves torn away
to crown both naked May and the wary fox at dawn
               posed glistening in the waste.

# Sandra Alcosser

∎

## WHAT MAKES THE GRIZZLIES DANCE

June and finally the snowpeas
sweeten in the Mission Valley.
High behind the numinous meadows
lady bugs swarm, like huge
lacquered fans from Hong Kong,
like the serrated skirts
of blown poppies,
whole mountains turn red.
And in the blue penstemon
the grizzly bears swirl
as they gaily bat the snaps
of color against their ragged mouths.
Have you never wanted to spin like that—
delirious on hairy, leathered feet
amidst the swelling berries
as you tasted the language
of early summer, shaping
the lazy operatic vowels,
cracking the hard-shelled
consonants like speckled
ruby insects between
your silver teeth?

# A Night on Goat Haunt

If you pack no meat, no perfume,
hang bells and heal all wounds,
there is a chance the grizzly
will let you sleep
        in his territory.

It is brilliant there, amethyst
and turquoise siltstone,
        sunset the colors
    of a salmon's belly
    grey around the edge.

The climb will make your eyes throb.
You will crave candles and whiskey,
but in the dark you cannot see
the shredded logs, the scat
of orange berries,
        only glaciers drifting closer
    by inches, blue-white water scalloped
    like moth wings.

Grizzlies walk the trail in green moonlight.
It's smoother, more silent. Dream-white
antelope float across your clearing,
tasting, marking footrocks.

The mountains by sunrise become a silver cradle.
You may sleep a few hours before departing.
Spiraling down with thirty pounds of tin and feathers
on your back, part of you will want
to remain. But as you cross the timberline
you'll see again mossy trees and strawberry blossoms.
        The glasslike fungus whose poison
    you could not name
will look delicious.

# Agha Shahid Ali

∎

## LEAVING SONORA

*living in the desert
has taught me to go inside myself
for shade*
—Richard Shelton

Certain landscapes insist on fidelity.
Why else would the poet of this desert
go inside himself for shade? Only
there do the perished tribes live.
The desert insists, always: Be faithful,
even to those who no longer exist.

The Hohokam lived here for 1500 years.
In his shade, the poet sees one of their women,
beautiful, her voice low as summer thunder.
Each night she saw, among the culinary ashes,
what the earth does only through a terrible pressure—
the fire, in minutes, transforming the coal into diamonds.

I left the desert at night—to return
to the East. From the plane I saw Tucson's lights
shatter into blue diamonds. My eyes dazzled
as we climbed higher: below a thin cloud,
and only for a moment, I saw those blue lights fade
into the outlines of a vanished village.

# A.R. Ammons

■

## DUNES

Taking root in windy sand
    is not an easy
way
to go about
    finding a place to stay.

A ditchbank or wood's-edge
    has firmer ground.

In a loose world though
    something can be started—
a root touch water,
    a tip break sand—

Mounds from that can rise
    on held mounds,
a gesture of building, keeping,
    a trapping
into shape.

Firm ground is not available ground.

# CORSONS INLET

I went for a walk over the dunes again this morning
to the sea,
then turned right along
   the surf
                rounded a naked headland
                and returned

  along the inlet shore:

it was muggy sunny, the wind from the sea steady and high,
crisp in the running sand,
    some breakthroughs of sun
  but after a bit

continuous overcast:

the walk liberating, I was released from forms,
from the perpendiculars,
    straight lines, blocks, boxes, binds
of thought
into the hues, shadings, rises, flowing bends and blends
        of sight:

                I allow myself eddies of meaning:
yield to a direction of significance
running
like a stream through the geography of my work:
  you can find
in my sayings
                swerves of action
                like the inlet's cutting edge:
           there are dunes of motion,
organizations of grass, white sandy paths of remembrance
in the overall wandering of mirroring mind:

but Overall is beyond me: is the sum of these events
I cannot draw, the ledger I cannot keep, the accounting
beyond the account:

in nature there are few sharp lines: there are areas of
primrose
    more or less dispersed;
disorderly orders of bayberry; between the rows
of dunes,
irregular swamps of reeds,
though not reeds alone, but grass, bayberry, yarrow, all . . .
predominantly reeds:

I have reached no conclusions, have erected no boundaries,
shutting out and shutting in, separating inside
            from outside: I have
            drawn no lines:
            as

manifold events of sand
change the dune's shape that will not be the same shape
tomorrow,

so I am willing to go along, to accept
the becoming
thought, to stake off no beginnings or ends, establish
            no walls:

by transitions the land falls from grassy dunes to creek
to undercreek: but there are no lines, though
      change in that transition is clear
      as any sharpness: but "sharpness" spread out,
allowed to occur over a wider range
than mental lines can keep:

the moon was full last night: today, low tide was low:
black shoals of mussels exposed to the risk
of air
and, earlier, of sun,

waved in and out with the waterline, waterline inexact,
caught always in the event of change:
      a young mottled gull stood free on the shoals
      and ate
to vomiting: another gull, squawking possession, cracked a crab,
picked out the entrails, swallowed the soft-shelled legs, a ruddy
turnstone running in to snatch leftover bits:

risk is full: every living thing in
siege: the demand is life, to keep life: the small
white blacklegged egret, how beautiful, quietly stalks and spears
            the shallows, darts to shore
                  to stab—what? I couldn't
      see against the black mudflats—a frightened
      fiddler crab?

            the news to my left over the dunes and
reeds and bayberry clumps was
            fall: thousands of tree swallows
            gathering for flight:
            an order held
            in constant change: a congregation
rich with entropy: nevertheless, separable, noticeable
      as one event,
            not chaos: preparations for

9

flight from winter,
cheet, cheet, cheet, cheet, wings rifling the green clumps,
beaks
at the bayberries
   a perception full of wind, flight, curve,
   sound:
   the possibility of rule as the sum of rulelessness:
the "field" of action
with moving, incalculable center:

in the smaller view, order tight with shape:
blue tiny flowers on a leafless weed: carapace of crab:
snail shell:
      pulsations of order
      in the bellies of minnows: orders swallowed,
broken down, transferred through membranes
to strengthen larger orders: but in the large view, no
lines or changeless shapes: the working in and out, together
     and against, of millions of events: this,
          so that I make
          no form of
          formlessness:

orders as summaries, as outcomes of actions override
or in some way result, not predictably (seeing me gain
the top of a dune,
the swallows
could take flight—some other fields of bayberry
     could enter fall
     berryless) and there is serenity:

     no arranged terror: no forcing of image, plan,
or thought:
no propaganda, no humbling of reality to precept:

terror pervades but is not arranged, all possibilities
of escape open: no route shut, except in
   the sudden loss of all routes:

     I see narrow orders, limited tightness, but will
not run to that easy victory:
     still around the looser, wider forces work:
     I will try
   to fasten into order enlarging grasps of disorder, widening
scope, but enjoying the freedom that
Scope eludes my grasp, that there is no finality of vision,
that I have perceived nothing completely,
     that tomorrow a new walk is a new walk.

# Ralph Angel

∎

## IT COULD HAVE BEEN MORE

In the sky above the clouds
nothing is falling. Lift and curl,
the wave's translucence. The pure blue sky
in the windows of bones,

by accident
the fold of the body, new skin for the wound.


And the clouds themselves, loose
and swept along. And the untouched rain
blowing through the empty rooms.
Was the need not always
for love, each loss

the same self breaking the heavens
into birds, birds into dark-massed trees?
I can't touch my own soul


though I know that I've dreamed it.
In a dream there are clothes, islands of
hair, snowdrifts flaring.
Boy child, dirty-faced and hopeful.
The woman who wakes up angry, overflowing,
grieving. Only one taste

in my mouth on the shoreline of brightness
and sky. Only one,
and the feelings I've drowned!

# Margaret Atwood

∎

## ELEGY FOR THE GIANT TORTOISES

Let others pray for the passenger pigeon
the dodo, the whooping crane, the eskimo:
everyone must specialize

I will confine myself to a meditation
upon the giant tortoises
withering finally on a remote island.

I concentrate in subway stations,
in parks, I can't quite see them,
they move to the peripheries of my eyes

but on the last day they will be there;
already the event
like a wave travelling shapes vision:

on the road where I stand they will materialize,
plodding past me in a straggling line
awkward without water

their small heads pondering
from side to side, their useless armour
sadder than tanks and history,

in their closed gaze ocean and sunlight paralysed,
lumbering up the steps, under the archways
toward the square glass altars

where the brittle gods are kept,
the relics of what we have destroyed,
our holy and obsolete symbols.

# Three Praises

**I**

The dipper, small dust-colored bird with robin
feet, walks on the stream bed
enclosed in its nimbus of silver
air, miraculous bubble, a non-miracle.
Who could have thought it? We think it now,
and liverwort on a dead log, earthstar,
hand, finger by finger.

**I**

For you, at last, I'd like to make
something uncomplicated; some neither god
nor goddess, not between, beyond
them; pinch it from dough,
bake it in the oven, a stone in its belly.
Stones lined up on the windowsill,
picked off some beach or other for being holy.

**I**

The hookworm, in the eye of
the universe, which is the unsteady gaze
of eternity maybe, is beloved. How could it not be,
living so blessed, in its ordained red meadows
of blood where it waves like a seaweed?
Praise be, it sings with its dracula mouth.
Praise be.

# Steven Bauer

∎

## WHITE CEDAR SWAMP

From the sea the trail snakes down through
  sassafras and pine, and as I go my fingers
    crush the oily mitten-shaped leaves and tapered

needles until I smell of root beer, turpentine,
  and pitch. I walk here once a week, a connoisseur
    of change, to see what's different: the new blunt

buds the swamp maple jabs at winter, another trunk
  tattooed by lichen, or the poofy brown-and-white
    unraveling of punk. But as the ground defers

to water, the trail to raised and weathered planks,
  I see again that here, nothing changes: the clear
    tea-colored water sifting its fraying deciduous carpet,

collars of ice restraining the eelgrass hammocks,
  the darting bright-eyed agitation of a waxwing,
    and over all, the evergreen fragrance of the cedars

fanning the aqueous light through their spatulate
  fingers. If I stand still I can hear the constant
    question of the ocean, and the land's broken reply:

almost like learning to wade, but tripping, falling,
  submerged, still touching bottom, before being pulled head-
    long into a wall of surf which never stops. My father took

my hand when I was a boy and helped me into the waves,
  then telling me to trust him, held me by my ankles above
    the whole white water-topped world; said *Don't be afraid.*

# Marvin Bell

∎

## THE SELF AND THE MULBERRY

I wanted to see the self, so I looked at the mulberry.
It had no trouble accepting its limits,
yet defining and redefining a small area
so that any shape was possible, any movement.
It stayed put, but was part of all the air.
I wanted to learn to be there and not there
like the continually changing, slightly moving
mulberry, wild cherry and particularly the willow.
Like the willow, I tried to weep without tears.
Like the cherry tree, I tried to be sturdy and productive.
Like the mulberry, I tried to keep moving.
I couldn't cry right, couldn't stay or go.
I kept losing parts of myself like a soft maple.
I fell ill like the elm. That was the end
of looking in nature to find a natural self.
Let nature think itself not manly enough!
Let nature wonder at the mystery of laughter.
Let nature hypothesize man's indifference to it.
Let nature take a turn at saying what love is!

# HEDGEAPPLE

1

I wish we'd gone back—
you didn't tell me she came off her porch
and ran through the green yards
waving us back as we drove away
but all the time in our blind spot.
That heavy fruit, the hedgeapple,
had made us stop. Then when she came waving
to the screen we flinched
a foot down on the gas pedal not to be
pinned for having intentions
on her hedgeapple tree.
She knew us,
she told you later,
but still we had the fear of correspondence,
and the guilt that comes from watching
someone else's treasure
in the open,
and also the fear of letting things be
more than they seem and ourselves less.
We should have gone back.

Do the trees really laugh?
Can we smell the light?
Is there smoke inside the cornstalk
and a light inside the tree,
a light that will not find where it came from?
What they call a hedgeapple—
it is one more perversion of the apple,
one more story like unto the ancient
unwilling airs and dances.
I am sure that we could have stolen one
and taken a bite apiece
and made ourselves crazy from the ground up.
We should have gone back.
We should have beckoned the wind
back into the hedgeapples
and her back in through the screen.

2

In spring, when the trees laugh,
like men and women who have been breathing
deeply and are also thirsty,
and the light
increases and increases
its waxy luxury so that a stand of bush
might seem an artist's wash,
we forget
what we were told.

First, the hedgeapple
is the giant birthing of a tree,
not a hedge, and second,
is no apple. A lemon grapefruit, maybe.
Like a grapefruit, but green.
Like an apple, but lemony.

We were lucky,
three in a car, the language we spoke
seeming to make light everywhere
because we stopped to look.
For a moment then, we forgot
what we were told.
And we didn't think.
Without us, the hedgeapple is perfect—
means nothing.
We should have gone back.
I am sure now she was watching us
from the beginning,
and the whole time too.

We thought we didn't take her hedgeapple.
We should have given it back.

So: here.

# Wendell Berry

∎

## MANIFESTO: THE MAD FARMER LIBERATION FRONT

Love the quick profit, the annual raise,
vacation with pay. Want more
of everything ready made. Be afraid
to know your neighbors and to die.
And you will have a window in your head.
Not even your future will be a mystery
any more. Your mind will be punched in a card
and shut away in a little drawer.
When they want you to buy something
they will call you. When they want you
to die for profit they will let you know.
So, friends, every day do something
that won't compute. Love the Lord.
Love the world. Work for nothing.
Take all that you have and be poor.
Love someone who does not deserve it.
Denounce the government and embrace
the flag. Hope to live in that free
republic for which it stands.
Give your approval to all you cannot
understand. Praise ignorance, for what man
has not encountered he has not destroyed.
Ask the questions that have no answers.
Invest in the millennium. Plant sequoias.
Say that your main crop is the forest
that you did not plant,
that you will not live to harvest.

Say that the leaves are harvested
when they have rotted into the mold.
Call that profit. Prophesy such returns.
Put your faith in the two inches of humus
that will build under the trees
every thousand years.
Listen to carrion—put your ear
close, and hear the faint chattering
of the songs that are to come.
Expect the end of the world. Laugh.
Laughter is immeasurable. Be joyful
though you have considered all the facts.
So long as women do not go cheap
for power, please women more than men.
Ask yourself: Will this satisfy
a woman satisfied to bear a child?
Will this disturb the sleep
of a woman near to giving birth?
Go with your love to the fields.
Lie easy in the shade. Rest your head
in her lap. Swear allegiance
to what is nighest your thoughts.
As soon as the generals and the politicos
can predict the motions of your mind,
lose it. Leave it as a sign
to mark the false trail, the way
you didn't go. Be like the fox
who makes more tracks than necessary,
some in the wrong direction.
Practice resurrection.

# Philip Booth

∎

## FOG

Winded, drifting to rest.
                               I'm rowing
between islands, between pewter water
and a gauze I'm unwinding that winds back
behind me in my flat wake.
                               At the tip
of each oar small vortices whorl
at each stroke's end.
                               If I looked down through
I could see Stephen who swam for his friend
on his eighth birthday. Or Mr. Ames,
swept overboard at daybreak, racing
big seas off Greenland. Or his boys
who went after him.
                               They were my heroes
the June I was nine. It's different now:
with no horizon, with the end
of the century coming up,
                               I'm rowing
where measure is lost, I'm barely moving,
in a circle of translucence that moves with me
without compass.
                               I can't see out or up into;
I sit facing backwards,
                               pulling myself slowly
toward the life I'm still trying to get at.

# How to See Deer

Forget roadside crossings.
Go nowhere with guns.
Go elsewhere your own way,

lonely and wanting. Or
stay and be early:
next to deep woods

inhabit old orchards.
All clearings promise.
Sunrise is good,

and fog before sun.
Expect nothing always;
find your luck slowly.

Wait out the windfall.
Take your good time
to learn to read ferns;

make like a turtle:
downhill toward slow water.
Instructed by heron,

drink the pure silence.
Be compassed by wind.
If you quiver like aspen

trust your quick nature:
let your ear teach you
which way to listen.

You've come to assume
protective color; now
colors reform to

new shapes in your eye.
You've learned by now
to wait without waiting;

as if it were dusk
look into light falling:
in deep relief

things even out. Be
careless of nothing. See
what you see.

# *Joseph Bruchac*

∎

## CATTAIL WIND

Go to the meadow behind Braim's pond
   when the day moves slow into night

Let the laughter of those
   who live by comparisons
lift from you like the mist
   now rising from the alders

The cattail wind feathers the evening
   shadows coalesce in the sky
beyond Orion's slanted belt
   cold fireflies of time
old messages for your eyes

If you wait long enough
two things will come

   the deer, eyes glowing
   with the valleys of the moon

   the dawn, uneven as
   the edge of wind-brushed feathers

They will touch your face
leave you
changed

This is no warning
   it is a map.

# Christopher Buckley

∎

## SPARROWS

Like the poor, they are with us always . . .
what they lack in beauty is theirs
in good cheer—tails like pump handles
lifting them first among songsters, chiding
citylight or roadside to evening's praise.
Gristmills, hardy gleaners, but for them
the weeds and thorns would find us wanting.
Ragmen to the wind, Sophists of the twig,
they pause to bathe in the ample dust
and accept the insect as relish to the seed.
So it is becoming to not be too fastidious
when you are rapidly inheriting the earth.

# Hayden Carruth

∎

## Essay

So many poems about the deaths of animals.
Wilbur's toad, Kinnell's porcupine, Eberhart's squirrel,
and that poem by someone—Hecht? Merrill?—
about cremating a woodchuck. But mostly
I remember the outrageous number of them,
as if every poet, I too, had written at least
one animal elegy; with the result that today
when I came to a good enough poem by Edwin Brock
about finding a dead fox at the edge of the sea
I could not respond; as if permanent shock
had deadened me. And then after a moment
I began to give way to sorrow (watching myself
sorrowlessly the while), not merely because
part of my being had been violated and annulled,
but because all these many poems over the years
have been necessary,—suitable and correct. This
has been the time of the finishing off of the animals.
They are going away—their fur and their wild eyes,
their voices. Deer leap and leap in front
of the screaming snowmobiles until they leap
out of existence. Hawks circle once or twice
around their shattered nests and then they climb
to the stars. I have lived with them fifty years,
we have lived with them fifty million years,
and now they are going, almost gone. I don't know
if the animals are capable of reproach.
But clearly they do not bother to say good-bye.

# Karen Chamberlain

∎

## STEPPING IN THE SAME RIVER

I wake to strangled voices
in the air. This is the hand
of August, this wedge
of wild geese delivering dawn

arrow by shadowed arrow to reeds
along the river. Mist rises
from the mud. Face cold, body
warm in a clammy sleeping bag,

I listen to the stream and feel
within me its surface leaping
in white waves unruly with joy,
while the gliding belly beneath

is raked by rock, snagged
by sunken log. Barefoot, cold,
I kneel on stones to wash
my face, and watch my image shatter

in a socket of empty sky. I brace
my foot in broken water. I have
been here before, thighs pressed
wet against chill rock

as I waded into this same eddy
on a January dawn years ago
to stop the slow, downriver spin
of a shot goose. My shot, my

prize. What the current presses
against me now is not
regret, not the gut turned inside out, but
gooseflesh—dry plumules holding

heat to my skin, the ordered poise
of bedded quills. Now I know
that silken rasp of wind against wingtip,
the sudden falter into icy water,
the limp neck in my hands as my own.

# Amy Clampitt

∎

## SEA MOUSE

The orphanage of possibility
has had to be expanded to
admit the sea mouse. No one
had asked for such a thing,
or prophesied its advent,

sheltering under ruching
edges of sea lettuce—
a wet thing but pettable
as, seen in the distance,
the tops of copses,

sun-honeyed, needle-pelted
pine trees, bearded barley,
or anything newborn not bald
but furred. No rodent this
scabrous, this unlooked-for

foundling, no catnip plaything
for a cat to worry, not even
an echinoderm, the creature
seems to be a worm. Silk-spiny,
baby-mummy-swaddled, it's

at home where every corridor
is mop-and-bucket scrubbed
and aired from wall to wall
twice daily by the inde-
fatigable tidal head nurse.

# NOTHING STAYS PUT

The strange and wonderful are too much with us.
The protea of the antipodes—a great,
globed, blazing honeybee of a bloom—
for sale in the supermarket! We are in
our decadence, we are not entitled.
What have we done to deserve
all the produce of the tropics—
this fiery trove, the largesse of it
heaped up like cannonballs, these pineapples, bossed
and crested, standing like troops at attention,
these tiers, these balconies of green, festoons
grown sumptuous with stoop labor?

The exotic is everywhere, it comes to us
before there is a yen or a need for it. The green-
grocers, uptown and down, are from South Korea.
Orchids, opulence by the pailful, just slightly
fatigued by the plane trip from Hawaii, are
disposed on the sidewalks; alstroemerias, freesias
fattened a bit in translation from overseas; gladioli
likewise estranged from their piercing ancestral crimson;
as well as, less altered from the original blue cornflower
of the roadsides and railway embankments of Europe, these
bachelor's buttons. But it isn't the railway embankments
their featherweight wheels of cobalt remind me of—it's

a row of them among prim colonnades of cosmos,
snapdragon, nasturtium, bloodsilk red poppies
in my grandmother's garden: a prairie childhood,
the grassland shorn, overlaid with a grid,
unsealed, furrowed, harrowed, and sown with immigrant grasses,
their massive corduroy, their wavering feltings embroidered
here and there by the scarlet shoulder patch of cannas
on a courthouse lawn, by a love knot, a cross-stitch
of living matter, sown and tended by women,
nurturers everywhere of the strange and wonderful,
beneath whose hands what had been alien begins,
as it alters, to grow as though it were indigenous.

But at this remove what I think of as
strange and wonderful—strolling the side streets of Manhattan
on an April afternoon, seeing hybrid pear trees in blossom,
a tossing, vertiginous colonnade of foam up above—
is the white petalfall, the warm snowdrift
of the indigenous wild plum of my childhood.
Nothing stays put. The world is a wheel.
All that we know, that we're
made of, is motion.

# Martha Collins

∎

## HOUSE, TREE, SKY

If, when the pond is still
and nothing is moved
and the light is right,
you consider the angles
and make the proper approach,
you come to a bend
where a small white house
against a deep sky meets
the same white house against
the blue water:
stair rests on stair,
door opens on door,
tree grows out of tree.
And if you steady your pace
and fix your eye on bough
or window or door you find
you're moving on a plane
and the depth you've lost
is the merest matter,
in the clear air ahead,
of up and down.
Walking a fine line
toward the intersecting
two-roofed house, you figure
you could be on the other
side and that could mean
both sides at once;
you think, without beginnings
ends or means you might
be getting to the point.
But just as you reach out
to open the door,
things begin to slip
beneath your feet:
the sky gets out from under,
the tree retrieves
its roots, the house recovers
its ground and you get down
to solid facts again.
Still, your recent loss
has made a difference:
looking around
you keep in mind the profound
surface of things.

# LAKE

It's in there somewhere.
It's coming over here, I thought,
as the lake licked the stony shore.

Listen now: a child
playing—no someone dusting
piano keys. Crescendo, diminuendo

of passing boat, passing—above
the still willows passing plane.
Silence. No: cicadas' slow vibrato

fades. Silence. No: hum
in the air, stir in the willows,
waves on the shore, it's coming

over here, I thought, but this
is it, taking it in, click
of a radio—*said the nation*—click

again, sudden sun sheds gold
on wave, illumines the vertical
script of willow, listen,

all attention now,
enter boat, cicada, lake, wade
the waves of sound light mind—

# RAIN

In the rain, the bark of the plane trees shines
in the colors, the shapes of camouflage:
trees looking like men looking like trees.

When the sun shines, the trees shade
the grass a darker green, the thick veins
of giant leaves, a giant's hands—

Terrain with deep cracks, that old puzzle—

In California, it rained on the queen
and the president, it rained on the good
and the bad, it rained on me.

In the jungle, it rains, it has rained,
it rains on the bodies fallen
like trees, on the bodies that walk.

In the rain, the shadows disappear.

In a larger rain, things are lost.

In the largest rains, borders emerge—

A puzzle coming apart, becoming the world.

# Douglas Crase

∎

## FROM THE REVISIONIST

If I could raise rivers, I'd raise them
Across the mantle of your past: old headwaters
Stolen, oxbows high and dry while new ones form,
A sediment of history rearranged. If I could unlock
The lakes, I'd spill their volume over the till
I know you cultivate: full accumulations swept away,
The habit of prairies turned to mud. If I had glaciers,
I'd carve at the stony cliffs of your belief:
Logical mountains lowered notch by notch, erratics
Dropped for you to stumble on. Earthquakes, and I'd
Seize your experience at its weakest edge: leveled
Along a fault of memories. Sunspots, I'd cloud
Your common sense; tides, and I'd drown its outlines
With a weight of water they could never bear.
If I had hurricanes, I'd worry your beaches
Into ambiguity: barrier islands to collect them
In one spot and in another the sudden gut
That sucks them loose to revolve in dispersion with
The waves. If I had frost, I'd shatter the backbone
Of your thought: an avalanche of gravel, a storm
Of dust. And if I could free volcanoes, I'd tap
The native energies you've never seen: counties
Of liquid rock to cool in summits you'd have to
Reckon from. If I could unroll a winter of time
When these were done, I'd lay around your feet
In endless fields where you could enter and belong,
A place returning and a place to turn to whole.

# IN MEMORY OF MY COUNTRY

As the land lifts
The weather begins at once to wear it down:
Its ridges lose their minerals in the rain,
Its valleys open in wide parallels. The hills
Sink of their own weight into plains, the plains
Sag into rivers of their own debris, and features
Hard as rocks will be transformed
To clouds of dust that drip out of the sky.
It is the land, as it appears,
That tells the world of time: conglomerate,
So fiercely made to pass through day and night,
Heaped up and gullied and borne away.
The falls cut upstream every year, the delta
Spreads, the breakers sort the sands
With no mistake. There is no place on earth
Hidden from earth's patient spin: the stumps
Of mountains turn in the same custody
As the worn plateau over which they rise.
Hard as granite, the weather levels the record
Of the toughest past whose moments unfasten
In confusion with the active land.

# Mary Crow

∎

## Fault-Finding

Even now the ground is slowly shifting
beneath your feet, accumulating strain
that must be released. Even now
zones of weakness are forming behind
your back, ready to turn
into fractures. Even now pressures
may exceed the ability of rocks
to resist. Think of it:
thousands of faults lace this region.
What is facing you is slowly cracking.
You live inside a ring of fire
where walls rise abruptly.
Forces in this landscape
can rearrange your world.
You stand there feeling
there is nothing you can control,
that at any second it is you
who may be heaved up, and broken.
No one will ever be able
to put you together again.

# *John Daniel*

∎

## COMMON GROUND

Everywhere on Earth, wet beginnings:

fur, feather, scale, shell, skin, bone, blood,

like an infant discovering sound after sound
a voice is finding its tongue
in the slop and squall of birth.

It sounds,

and we, in whom Earth chose to light
a clear flame of consciousness,
are only beginning to learn the language—

who are made of the ash of stars,
who carry the sea we were born in,
who spent millions of years learning to breathe,
who shivered in fur at the reptiles' feet,
who trained eyes and hands in the trees
and came down, slowly straightening
to look over the grasses, to see
that the world not only is
                              but is beautiful—

we are Earth learning to see itself,
to hear, touch, and taste. What it wants to be
no one knows: finding a way
in starlight and dark, it begins in beauty,
                              it asks only time.

# THE UNBORN

*for David Brower*

Whatever they could be
we hold in seed—
their faces
containing our faces
in the darkness deeper
than anyone can remember,
their voices
that given speech
will speak for us
when we have passed beyond speech—
whatever it is
the world wants to become
only they can tell,
only in them
can the womb say its name
and only in us
can they speak at all,
they speak
if we speak for them.

# Alison Deming

■

## CANOEING THE SALT MARSH
Scarborough, Maine

All eels migrate to the Sargasso
to breed, the guide says, dragging
fingers like a seine behind the canoe
to catch the feel of the tidal stream,
sense the shimmer of a species
coming together in January.

July now. Last year's offspring
lounge under mats of algae,
filter the peat-flecked stream
through gills and wait to be stirred.

Blades of grass glisten in the sanctuary.

Osprey.  Black-back.  Herring gull.

Scanning the tapestry of greens,
I want to know the one grass
that survives by extruding salt
along its glittering spine.
Bivalves too adapt. Submerged
three days in sterile tanks,
they pump themselves clean of coliform,
then leave the stocky Blue Point factory—
sweet, minced and canned.

The Penobscots came to that point
to dig and dry clams enough
to last the inland winter
that tucked underneath the scrubby pines.

Their sanctuary was endless.

Jackpine, jack rabbit, jack-in-the-pulpit,

where now the subdivided county
sleeps outside the fence
that keeps the salt marsh safe
and SAC planes overhead
drag thunder through the perfect sky.

Moving with the outgoing tide,
flotsam of microbes and mica-lit sand, moving
toward the prayer that everything is praying,
I wake up with the eels at the blood-call.

# DREAMWORK WITH HORSES

Last night I dreamed again about the horse
and for once I knew that what I miss
is not the false arcadia of the family farm
where lambs are born with no blood on their faces,
but something wild and vengeful inside,
ignored, now demanding to be fed.

∎

Weeks pass when I forget the chores
until it occurs to me like a siren
that the animal must be dead. I rush back
to the pasture. The horse ambles up,
buzzing her lips in contentment, no thinner
than I left her. It's clear she doesn't need me,
though I'm sick of myself for forgetting.

∎

When the horse comes into my suburban house,
it suddenly seems possible to keep her
no matter where I live. I lead her out
the kitchen door for a ride, but barefoot
must go back for boots. Her bridle, jury-rigged
baling twine, is too weak to hitch her outside.
So I lead her back up the porch stairs, inside,
then out, less afraid of injury than of losing
my connection, the possibility of riding
full-tilt across the hayfield.

∎

Even in my wildest dream the horse comes out on top.
Two horses battle, the stallion knocked out,
then men interceding while the herd grazes nervously,
roan, chestnut and bay shining the most beautifully
as if groomed and curried by their own aggression.
They got rid of the cowboy—the stubbled, hard-denim man
hit the electrified fence, flew into the air like a back-lit cloud.

∎

I spent months trying to solve this dream,
as if I were the troubled adolescent
who raged through a stable stabbing out
the eyes of his passion
for the distortion of civilized love—
what waking does to the dream
when what I wanted was to remain faithful to its clarity.

# James Dickey

∎

## FOR THE LAST WOLVERINE

They will soon be down

To one, but he still will be
For a little while   still will be stopping

The flakes in the air with a look,
Surrounding himself with the silence
Of whitening snarls. Let him eat
The last red meal of the condemned

To extinction, tearing the guts

From an elk. Yet that is not enough
For me. I would have him eat

The heart, and, from it, have an idea
Stream into his gnawing head
That he no longer has a thing
To lose, and so can walk

Out into the open, in the full

Pale of the sub-Artic sun
Where a single spruce tree is dying

Higher and higher. Let him climb it
With all his meanness and strength.
Lord, we have come to the end
Of this kind of vision of heaven,

As the sky breaks open

Its fans around him and shimmers
And into its northern gates he rises

Snarling   complete   in the joy of a weasel
With an elk's horned heart in his stomach
Looking straight into the eternal
Blue, where he hauls his kind. I would have it all

My way: at the top of that tree I place

The New World's last eagle
Hunched in mangy feathers   giving

Up on the theory of flight.

Dear God of the wildness of poetry, let them mate
To the death in the rotten branches,
Let the tree sway and burst into flame

And mingle them, crackling with feathers,

In crownfire. Let something come
Of it   something gigantic   legendary

Rise beyond reason over hills
Of ice   SCREAMING   that it cannot die,
That it has come back, this time
On wings, and will spare no earthly thing:

That it will hover, made purely of northern

Lights, at dusk   and fall
On men building roads: will perch

On the moose's horn like a falcon
Riding into battle   into holy war against
Screaming railroad crews: will pull
Whole traplines like fibres from the snow

In the long-jawed night of fur trappers.

But, small, filthy, unwinged,
You will soon be crouching

Alone, with maybe some dim racial notion
Of being the last, but none of how much
Your unnoticed going will mean:
How much the timid poem needs

The mindless explosion of your rage,

The glutton's internal fire   the elk's
Heart in the belly, sprouting wings,

The pact of the "blind swallowing
Thing," with himself, to eat
The world, and not to be driven off it
Until it is gone, even if it takes

Forever. I take you as you are

And make of you what I will,
Skunk-bear, carcajou, bloodthirsty

Non-survivor.
                    *Lord, let me die   but not die*
*Out.*

# The Heaven of Animals

Here they are. The soft eyes open.
If they have lived in a wood
It is a wood.
If they have lived on plains
It is grass rolling
Under their feet forever.

Having no souls, they have come,
Anyway, beyond their knowing.
Their instincts wholly bloom
And they rise.
The soft eyes open.

To match them, the landscape flowers,
Outdoing, desperately
Outdoing what is required:
The richest wood,
The deepest field.

For some of these,
It could not be the place
It is, without blood.
These hunt, as they have done,
But with claws and teeth grown perfect,

More deadly than they can believe.
They stalk more silently,
And crouch on the limbs of trees,
And their descent
Upon the bright backs of their prey

May take years
In a sovereign floating of joy.
And those that are hunted
Know this as their life,
Their reward: to walk

Under such trees in full knowledge
Of what is in glory above them,
And to feel no fear,
But acceptance, compliance.
Fulfilling themselves without pain

At the cycle's center,
They tremble, they walk
Under the tree,
They fall, they are torn,
They rise, they walk again.

# Norman Dubie

∎

## ELEGY TO THE SIOUX

The vase was made of clay
With spines of straw
For strength. The sun-baked vase
Soaked in a deep blue dye for days. The events in this wilderness,
Portrayed in the round of the vase,

Depend on shades of indigo against
The masked areas of the clay, a flat pearl color
To detail the big sky and snow . . .

This Montana field in winter is not sorrowful:
A bugle skips through notes:

We view it all somehow from the center of the field
And there are scattered groups of cavalry. Some of these
Men were seasoned by civil war. Their caps are blue.
Their canteens are frozen. The horses shake their heads
Bothered by the beads of ice, the needles of ice
Forming at both sides of their great anvil heads.

The long, blue cloaks of the officers fall over the haunches
Of the horses. The ammunition wagons
Beside the woods are blurred by the snowy weather . . .

Beyond the wagons, further even, into the woods
There is a sloping stream bed. This is
The dark side of the vase, which is often misunderstood.
From here through the bare trees there's
A strange sight to be seen at the very middle of the field:

A valet is holding a bowl of cherries—archetype and rubric,
A general with white hair eats the fruit while introducing its color,
Which will flow through the woods in early December.
An Indian woman came under dark clouds to give birth, unattended
In the deep wash inside the woods. She knew the weather

Could turn and staked the tips of two rooted spruce trees
To the earth to make a roof.
The deerskin of her robe is in her mouth. Her legs spread,
Her feet are tied up in the roof of darkening spruce. *No stars
Show through!* But on the vase that belonged to a President
There are countless stars above the soldier's campfires . . .

With rawhide her feet are tied high in the spruce
And her right hand is left loose as if she were about
To ride a wild stallion
                              to its conclusion in a box canyon.


President Grant drinks bourbon from his boot. The Sioux
Cough in their blankets . . .


It snowed an hour more, and then the moon appeared.
The unborn infant,
Almost out on the forest floor, buckled and lodged. It died.
Its mother died. Just before she closed her eyes
She rubbed snow up and down the inside of her bare thighs.

In the near field an idle, stylish horse raised one leg
To make a perfect right angle. Just then a ghost of snow formed
Over the tents of the soldiers,

It blows past the stylish, gray horse,
Unstopped it moves through woods, up the stream bed
And passes into the crude spruce shelter, into the raw open
Woman, her legs raised into sky—
Naked house of snow and ice! This gust of wind

Spent the night within the woman. At sunrise, it left her mouth
Tearing out trees, keeping the owls from sleep; it was angry now
And into the field it spilled, into the bivouac of pony soldiers
Who turned to the south, who turned back to the woods, who became

Still. Blue all over! If there is snow
Still unspooling in the mountains
Then there is time yet for the President to get his Indian vase
And to fill it with bourbon from his boot and to put flowers into it:
The flowers die in a window that looks out on a cherry tree
Which heavy with fruit drops a branch:
                              torn to its very heartwood
By the red clusters of fruit, the branch fell
Like her leg and foot
Out of the big sky into Montana . . .

# Stephen Dunn

∎

## From Underneath

*A giant sea turtle saved the life
of a 52 year old woman lost at sea
for two days after a shipwreck
in the Southern Philippines. She rode
on the turtle's back.*

—Syracuse Post-Standard

When her arms were no longer
strong enough to tread water
it came up beneath her, hard
and immense, and she thought
this is how death comes,
something large between your legs
and then the plunge.
She dived off instinctively,
but it got beneath her again
and when she realized what it was
she soiled herself, held on.

God would have sent something winged,
she thought. *This* came from beneath,
a piece of hell that killed a turtle
on the way and took its shape.
How many hours passed?
She didn't know, but it was night
and the waves were higher.
The thing swam easily in the dark.

She swooned into sleep.
When she woke it was morning,
the sea calm, her strange raft
still moving. She noticed the elaborate
pattern of its shell, map-like,
the leathery neck and head
as if she'd come up behind
an old longshoreman
in a hard-backed chair.
She wanted and was afraid to touch
the head—one finger
just above the eyes—
the way she could touch her cat
and make it hers.
The more it swam a steady course

the more she spoke to it
the jibberish of the lost.
And then the laughter
located at the bottom
of oneself, unstoppable.

The call went from sailor to sailor
on the fishing boat: A woman
riding an "oil drum"
off the starboard side.
But the turtle was already swimming
toward the prow
with its hysterical, foreign cargo
and when it came up alongside
it stopped
until she could be hoisted off.
Then it circled three times
and went down.
The woman was beyond all language,
the captain reported;
the crew was afraid of her
for a long, long time.

# Russell Edson

∎

## THE ADVENTURES OF A TURTLE

The turtle carries his house on his back. He is both the house and the person of that house.

But actually, under the shell is a little room where the true turtle, wearing long underwear, sits at a little table. At one end of the room a series of levers sticks out of slots in the floor, like the controls of a steam shovel. It is with these that the turtle controls the legs of his house.

Most of the time the turtle sits under the sloping ceiling of his turtle room reading catalogues at the little table where a candle burns. He leans on one elbow, and then the other. He crosses one leg, and then the other. Finally he yawns and buries his head in his arms and sleeps.

If he feels a child picking up his house he quickly douses the candle and runs to the control levers and activates the legs of his house and tries to escape.

If he cannot escape he retracts the legs and withdraws the so-called head and waits. He knows that children are careless, and that there will come a time when he will be free to move his house to some secluded place, where he will relight his candle, take out his catalogues and read until at last he yawns. Then he'll bury his head in his arms and sleep. . . . That is, until another child picks up his house. . . .

# *John Engels*

∎

## CARDINALS

1

I saw the cardinal
from the kitchen window
on one of the first warm days:
a scarlet puff at the center

of the holly bush, a red,
beaked, and black-eyed berry.
His crest lifted
to the wind. I tapped the glass,

but it was only when I walked out
and reached into the bush
so that I was no more
than five inches from taking him

into the circle of my thumb and finger
where I thought he might burn
like a small, beating flame,
that suddenly he sleeked

and flickered low across the yard
into the heart of a dark cedar.

2

The lawns were full
of green light. There was
a scarlet litter
of windfall holly berries.

Five feeding cardinals
bloomed in the grass. It was
a day for the felling of trees,
the butchering of animals,

the capture of great fish.
But I looked into the cold
blue iris of the sky,
I saw that although

I had been set upright,
I would be permitted
to fall back.

# Louise Erdrich

∎

## I Was Sleeping Where the Black Oaks Move

We watched from the house
as the river grew, helpless
and terrible in its unfamiliar body.
Wrestling everything into it,
the water wrapped around trees
until their life-hold was broken.
They went down, one by one,
and the river dragged off their covering.

Nests of the herons, roots washed to bones,
snags of soaked bark on the shoreline:
a whole forest pulled through the teeth
of the spillway. Trees surfacing
singly, where the river poured off
into arteries for fields below the reservation.

When at last it was over, the long removal,
they had all become the same dry wood.
We walked among them, the branches
whitening in the raw sun.
Above us drifted herons,
alone, hoarse-voiced, broken,
settling their beaks among the hollows.

Grandpa said, *These are the ghosts of the tree people,
moving above us, unable to take their rest.*

Sometimes now, we dream our way back to the heron dance.
Their long wings are bending the air
into circles through which they fall.
They rise again in shifting wheels.
How long must we live in the broken figures
their necks make, narrowing the sky.

# Phillip Foss

∎

## FROM VIRGA. ICY GATE.

The land lulls and consumes.
And confuses us with its brittle rhymes.
The fantastic hunt perpetuated
Will lead us back
Permitted to delineate space.
There is a single crow perched
Centered exactly between nowhere
Is that of a man suffocating.
And sleep,
To believe its rage is equal
And we leave it

The relentless voice assails
We have hope
by this belief
to the spare vegetation
But invariably
upon a telephone pole
and its voice
It suggests night
but we are not allowed
to our belief in flight,
and the air to themselves.


Brilliant light attests
Float by recklessly.
Into the wash. We would taste
Bury ourselves to be resurrected
The landscape is strewn
Of our failure.
In the last laughter
Snow heaves toward us
The sky reels.
Smiling, remembering
And thin as brush smoke
Blowing south

to our dissent. The seasons
Blossoms have fallen
the land with fullness,
with knowledge.
with relics
A black widow ruminates
of the beer can.
as benevolent as stone;
We awaken in the borrow-pit,
we dreamt we could fly.
we hear the voices of geese
along the blue mountains.

# Carol Frost

∎

## THE SNAKE SKINS

The intrigue of this house
is a snake in the foundation, disturbed once
out of his stone place
by a laborer who was removing part of the floor

and southern wall, its lath and crumbling plaster,
to add a sliding glass door.
There were five or six shed skins,
like a multiplication

of the snake's slithering
so close beneath the whispers the night
provoked us to hear and our bare feet.
Now, though more variance of light

pours into the century-old house, flux
and equinox,
and though the laborer cut in half the snake,
I think in darkness, deep in the recesses

of air and dust, in edifices
thought solid, of the little motions
going on, breeding snakes that may
and may

not be meek. I only know
of the spotted adder dead long ago
and these skins like gloves for individual fingers.
I suspect there are others.

# To Kill a Deer

Into the changes of autumn brush
the doe walked, and the hide, head and ears
were the tinsel browns. They made her.
I could not see her. She reappeared, stuffed with apples,
and I shot her. Into the pines she ran,
and I ran after. I might have lost her,
seeing no sign of blood or scuffle,
but felt myself part of the woods,
a woman with a doe's ears, and heard her
dying, counted her last breaths like a song
of dying, and found her dying.
I shot her again because her eyes
were open, and her lungs rattled like castanets,
then poked her with the gun barrel
because her eyes were dusty and unreal.
I opened her belly and pushed the insides
like rotted fruit into a rabbit hole,
skinned her, broke her leg joints under my knee,
took the meat, smelled the half-digested smell
that was herself. Ah, I closed her eyes.
I left her refolded in some briars
with the last sun on her head
like a benediction, head tilted on its axis
of neck and barren bone; head bent
wordless over a death, though I heard
the night wind blowing through her fur,
heard riot in the emptied head.

# THE LANDSCAPES

Watch them. The landscapes. That urge, glory
before the roar of each new surf; what goes on
before the plowman tames the jumbled hills
or points the wind. Move to the edge
of the room, let the others pass. No guide
will help you see. No dates or "middle periods."
It must be with the sense
of utter lonesomeness, yourself walking to the mountain
or lying under the pear tree's wild whites and viridians.
You look at a sunset sometimes,
and you know you've never seen it,
the quarry's living glare before bursting for cover.
Look now! Is something caught here? How to hold
creation in the eyes. How to savor,
before Eden made bestial and common glory
man's sorrow, the mountains, sea, hawk, leaf mold,
rotting bark. And no trace of anecdote.

# Brendan Galvin

∎

## COUGAR

Non-native plantings stuck into lawns,
welded chain supporting the mailboxes,
too many electives at the regional
school—we were in danger
until a state trooper saw it
pad with dignity across the road
in his headlights, and the dark
around here became furred
with something more than frost.
Some are betting that it's
what jumps electric fence
to ride pigs bareback, going for
the neck, digging in along the flanks,
printing a five-foot stride,
and that it's wearing a collar
because a camper let it out
when it got too big for his van,
but nobody's playing expert
with this mystery, though
they're reaching back for stories.
Good to know we have places
the houselights don't pin down,
so the slick-magazine man from Boston
can stop speculating about
our drinking habits; good to feel,
going from car to porchlight,
the short hairs lifting off my neck.

# James Galvin

∎

## EVERYONE KNOWS WHOM THE SAVED ENVY

It isn't such a bad thing,
To live in one world forever.
You could do a lot worse:
The sexual smell of fresh-cut alfalfa
Could well be missing somewhere.
Somewhere you'd give in to some impetuous unknown,
And then stand guilty, as accused, of self-love.
It's better not to take such risks.

It's not as if we had no angels:
A handful remained when the rest moved on.
Now they work for a living,
As windmills on the open range.
They spin and stare like catatonics,
Nod toward the bedridden peaks.
They've learned their own angelic disbelief.

The mountains still breathe, I suppose,
Though barely.
The prairie still swells under a few small churches.
They are like rowboats after the ship's gone down.
Everyone knows whom the saved envy.
Runoff mirrors the sky in alpine pastures;
Imagine how quickly one's tracks unbloom there.
This world isn't such a bad world.

At least the angels are gainfully employed:
They know where the water is,
What to do with wind.
I try not to think of those others,
Like so many brides,
So many owls made of pollen
Wintering in a stand of imaginary timber.

# Brewster Ghiselin

∎

## RATTLESNAKE

I found him sleepy in the heat
And dust of a gopher burrow,
Coiled in loose folds upon silence
In a pit of the noonday hillside.
I saw the wedged bulge
Of the head hard as a fist.
I remembered his delicate ways:
The mouth a cat's mouth yawning.
I crushed him deep in dust,
And heard the loud seethe of life
In the dead beads of the tail
Fade, as wind fades
From the wild grain of the hill.

## THE CATCH

The track of a broad rattler, dragged over dust at dawn, led us
Across the flats of morning under mesquite and paloverdes,
Path direct as hunger, up to a heaped grace of shade
Rodents had riddled into a hill of galleries. There it ended.

We dug into dust to take alive a lord of venom, whole
Rope and writhe as thick as a child's thigh, in halls of his Hell.

But what we found, under a crust crumpling to knives of spades,
Was a path of fury: earth as light and loose as a harrow beds,
Smell of plowland cut and clawed, and darker down in the mound
A sprawling rag of dragon's pearly armor slubbered with mud.

The feasting grave trembled. It shook us. We heard the darkness grunt.
A snout full of snarls, of a hound or a hog, heaved the spade up and dug
    under.

But was stopped in its tunneling by the steel, as steel was stopped in its
    teeth. It turned
Quick, clawing and snapping up light, it charged and a choker rolled it at
    pole's end
A badger strap-throttled, flipping like a marlin, battling like a bull on a
    gaff
And snoring anger till over his bravery and scuffling the door of a cage
    clapped.

Burrowing bearclaws rattled in tin. He tasted wire all round.
He bucked, he bruised the ceiling, lunged at a beam and was eating
      oakwood.

But for that ravening he lived unfed and unslaked. His stench was
      immense,
His dung was the curved needle ribs of reptiles. He never slept—
Daylong, nightlong. His furious freedom resounded. At starlit dawn
Jaws and claws rasping and thudding thump of his thunder drummed
      once. Long

Silences rang for him, cage-eater greedy of snakes, abroad in the dawn.


## Song at San Carlos Bay

Poled high on his cactus over a cliff of desert island, the osprey
Dipping his head at leisure slivers quivering silver, alive
A long while; then settling erect to stillness whitens his breast to the sun.

Slow waves flow in from the open distance and arm of ocean, bright sea
      of Cortés,
And over the tiderock under my cliff the white of the ebb rises and spreads
Thinning along the brown of the rock and down to the gathering trough
      of its fall.

∎

If there are other worlds (there may be—must be—amid the billion trillions,
And more, of the stars) they cannot be wholly as this one is: the torrent of
      the galaxy
Falling—as I saw it today before dawn—down the whole height of the
      dark to the ocean
Could not be as here, that momentary mist of a cataract so slowly floating
      it seems
Unchanged forever, the same after fifty years as I saw it when first its light
Untangled to curve and cluster in constellations, Scorpio, Sagittarius, sea
      stars
The crickets of a cliff long crumbled landward and blind with houselights
      cried under and are quiet.

∎

High on his cactus cliff the osprey leaning to unfold
His flight to the wind floats opening the forms of his motion flowing
And rises away to beat the light of his vantage and to fall.

La Montaña Encantada, high westward blunted with cloud, is sharpening
      its stone to the sun.

∎

As for those other worlds, islands ranging the waste alive
Like ours in the sway of a sun, I see—for analogy is blind to reveal them—
Only how each from our own and all from all of the others may differ,
Vastly in aspect, little in the mode of their ordering, alike as the stars are.

∎

To the osprey the span of the osprey is sufficient. Even in its moment
Of engendering, the germ of the life of the bird is unfolding wings
And hackling a ninefold hook to hang the blood of the sea
On the thorny air. So I in the instant of embrace that began me
Was opening my arms, to love and death, and my eyes to a vast.

∎

Where is the end of space? a child said, to the infinite iterations of the
    crickets,
To the tangle of his stars. How is there an end of it? Or how no end?
    "It is space
All the way out. . . ." No answer, but abundance—hard horn of dilemma
    broken
By absurdity to sweetness, antinomies darkening to restore to us the
    enormity of night.

∎

If being is the heart of that mystery—as it is of ours, who are in it and of it—
Its truth is not chanted in the noon of the grasshoppers or measured in the
    spangle of our stars,
But in silence and darkness: in deliverance from the figure of an image,
    our own in presumption,
Familiar of voice or face, or other particular of light to configure it,
Ground and palm and nest of fire, to reveal it in the mode of its ordering. . . .

It could not, I think, be narrow as purpose is—so careless and so careful:
Careless of all but itself, slitting its fish tail-first, though anguish
Quiver with double force, of life and of death-throe, careful and sure
To hold with hooks what is purely its own sweetness and never to relinquish.

∎

Evening begins, with a darkening of blue on the sea and a darkening of
    shadow on the rockroost,
The island of birds. The sun is yet high, the clouds are the same—
    hesitations of wings.
And no bird descends but to feed. The gannets will swing and drop to the
    water until dusk.
The spouting foam of the pelicans' fall on the swarming waves will detonate
    like depthcharges,
An hour or more, till planets hover the west, and the stars that are veiled
    with light,
Canopus over the sea, Sirius, and Rigel of Orion, are hiding the dark.

# *Margaret Gibson*

∎

## DOING NOTHING

I balance
on one foot, then the other,
reaching in for the pebbly berries
suspended on red whips and canes,
a lush clinging. On edge,
I reach in, the hone of a thorn
not unlike the whine
of mosquitoes beneath the leaves.
I pick my way in,
as if this discipline
has nothing to do with the moon
which last night opened
red, then paled
to the pale of a petal
in a still, black sky.
Slowly I pick my way in,
skillfully, a means that
has nothing to do with
doing harm
or with harvest.

For this moment, I forget
the pain that wants to
forget pain, and practice
touching lightly.
I watch my hands learn
their way past each
edge, each horizon,
lightly, touching
until between each berry
there is such space
I no longer have to hold
back, let go, or grasp.
Doing nothing, I
no longer wait for whole
other worlds to break open,
more beautiful than this one
whose wild darkness
stains my fingers,
my mouth, my tongue.

# Greg Glazner

∎

## FISHING: THE LATE WISH

The frozen shallows, weighted
with two weeks of snow, lay silent
at each bank, as my breathing
steamed that speechless afternoon away.

Thigh-deep in heavy waders,
I'd waited hours for the water
to reveal a winter brown. No motion
in the pools, no current-flash

or thrashing, but a few enormous flakes
were falling. I half-believed the crows,
whose calls were muffled, lovely
above the drifted hills, might swirl down

with the snow, and dissolve
into that frigid, empty rolling.
And as ice began to pearl
the eyelets of my rod, and the lure,

for hours, fell unbidden
to each swell and freezing stillness,
I understood how a living fisherman
could long to lie back there

and let the river drift him
past all knowing, so the vault of days
could glaze away his face's hollows,
encrust the risen tips of his boots,

and float the polished emblem of a body
fusing with ice floes, shrouded whiter
in each snow, silent to the marrow
with the perfection of the January cold.

# Louise Glück

∎

## ALL HALLOWS

Even now this landscape is assembling.
The hills darken. The oxen
sleep in their blue yoke,
the fields having been
picked clean, the sheaves
bound evenly and piled at the roadside
among cinquefoil, as the toothed moon rises:

This is the barrenness
of harvest or pestilence.
And the wife leaning out the window
with her hand extended, as in payment,
and the seeds
distinct, gold, calling
*Come here*
*Come here, little one*

And the soul creeps out of the tree.

## THANKSGIVING

They have come again to graze the orchard,
knowing they will be denied.
The leaves have fallen; on the dry ground
the wind makes piles of them, sorting
all it destroys.

What doesn't move, the snow will cover.
It will give them away; their hooves
make patterns which the snow remembers.
In the cleared field, they linger
as the summoned prey whose part
is not to forgive. They can afford to die.
They have their place in the dying order.

# Ray Gonzalez

∎

## EASTER SUNDAY 1988, THE GRAND CANYON, ARIZONA

Bodies are resurrected
as the whole earth opens
to show how far we must fall
to keep falling,
how deeply we must fear
the savage god
that tears the distance
into red miles of a planet
we will never reach,
the other side of fear
we will never climb because
the trail to the bottom
leads to the tomb of the river
where the earth continues
to eat itself,

feeding upon the river
that devours the river
until bodies rise
in their own space
to float miles across a canyon
that is not a landscape,
but remains of a great prayer
whose chant cut hundreds of miles
of rock into one big tomb
where bodies suddenly
start falling again,
descending to the bottom
of the inner atmospheres
where gravity grabs us
off the rim,
the river rising to meet us
the last thing we ever see.

# *Jorie Graham*

∎

## WANTING A CHILD

How hard it is for the river here to re-enter
the sea, though it's most beautiful, of course, in the waste
of time where it's almost
turned back. Then
it's yoked,
trussed. . . . The river
has been everywhere, imagine, dividing, discerning,
cutting deep into the parent rock,
scouring and scouring
its own bed.
Nothing is whole
where it has been. Nothing
remains unsaid.
Sometimes I'll come this far from home
merely to dip my fingers in this glittering, archaic
sea that renders everything
identical, flesh
where mind and body
blur. The seagulls squeak, ill-fitting
hinges, the beach is thick
with shells. The tide
is always pulsing upward, inland, into the river's rapid
argument, pushing
with its insistent tragic waves—the living echo,
says my book, of some great storm far out at sea, too far
to be recalled by us
but transferred
whole onto this shore by waves, so that erosion
is its very face.

# Linda Gregg

∎

## PRAISING SPRING

The day is taken by each thing and grows complete.
I go out and come in and go out again,
confused by a beauty that knows nothing of delay,
rushing like fire. All things move faster
than time and make a stillness thereby. My mind
leans back and smiles, having nothing to say.
Even at night I go out with a light and look
at the growing. I kneel and look at one thing
at a time. A white spider on a peony bud.
I have nothing to give, and make a poor servant,
but I can praise the spring. Praise this wildness
that does not heed the hour. The doe that does not
stop at dark but continues to grow all night long.
The beauty in every degree of flourishing. Violets
lift to the rain and the brook gets louder than ever.
The old German farmer is asleep and the flowers go on
opening. There are stars. Mint grows high. Leaves
bend in the sunlight as the rain continues to fall.

# John Haines

∎

## INTO THE GLACIER

With the green lamp of the spirit
of sleeping water
taking us by the hand . . .

Deeper and deeper,
a luminous blackness opening
like the wings of a raven—

as though a heavy wind
were rising through all the houses
we ever lived in—

the cold rushing in,
our blankets flying away
into the darkness,
and we, naked and alone,
awakening forever . . .


## THE TUNDRA

The tundra is a living
body, warm in the grassy
autumn sun; it gives off
the odor of crushed
blueberries and gunsmoke.

In the tangled lakes
of its eyes a mirror of ice
is forming, where
frozen gut-piles shine
with a dull, rosy light.

Coarse, laughing men
with their women;
one by one the tiny campfires
flaring under the wind.

Full of blood, with a sound
like clicking hoofs,
the heavy tundra slowly
rolls over and sinks
in the darkness.

# In the Forest Without Leaves

Before any match was struck
or a candle lighted,
someone spoke well of the sun.

There were bones to read
while the long dusk lasted,
marrow to force with a stick.

Feather of auk, beak of owl,
were tools to work the shadows,
make the winter hawk fly
and the stone ox stand.

As sparks fly seaward
from a beaten driftlog,
telling the days of a journey . . .

So from its mitten a hand
cracked with frost
parted the mosswick flame,
to read in a shoulderblade
the source of smoke
and meaning of the wind.

Nothing was written for the snow
to keep or the water
to carry, nothing to be forgotten.

And one man late in his years,
by light of the sun
through a wall of ice,
carved from ivory
a weasel the length of his finger.

1977–83

∎

This earth written over with words,
with names, and the names
come out of the ground,
the words like spoken seeds.

What field, what dust,
what namesake for a stone
that moves by inches
and clears a path in the mud?

Ice moved once, a river of stones,
and the road it drove
through the forest can still be walked.
Look there—you will find
for your house a standing boulder.

Earth worn deep by its names,
written over with words:

There are spaces inside those words,
and silence for the clearing
where no house stands.

1977

∎


How the sun came to the forest:

How the rain spoke
and the green branch flowered:

How the moss burned
and the wasp took flight,
how the sun in a halo of smoke
put an end to summer.

How the wind blew
and the leaves fell.

Death made a space in the forest
where snow would come,
and silence, and night.

1984

∎

In all the forest, chilled
by its spent wealth,

in the killed kingdom of grass
where birch leaves
tumble and blow;

(and over the leaves is written:
how great the harvest,
how deep the plow)

I know one truth:

Nothing stains like blood,
nothing whitens like snow.

1978–84

∎


What will be said of you,
tree of life,
when the final axe-blow
sends your great wood crashing?

Something about the wind upstairs,
that tromping and thrashing
on a roof never still?

What of the rift in your rafters
parting, your nests
and shingles flying?

What trace of your winter shadow,
but a lean, fantastic spider
sprawled and knotted in the snow?

And no one left to tell
of your heartwood
peeled down to a seed of ash,
your crowned solitude
crushed to a smouldering knot . . .

The ages parted to let you fall,
and a tall star blazed.

1978–84

∎

In the forest without leaves
stands a birch tree,
slender and white.

For the sun drank pallor
from its leaves,
and the marrow in its roots
froze down.

Only the paper bark stayed
to weather and peel,
be sunlight or tinder
burned in the hunter's fire,

and wind took away all the rest.

If and whenever we come again,
I will know that tree.

A birch leaf held fast
in limestone ten million years
still quietly burns,
though claimed by the darkness.

Let earth be this windfall
swept to a handful of seeds—
one tree, one leaf,
gives us plenty of light.

1977–84

# Donald Hall

∎

## Names of Horses

All winter your brute shoulders strained against collars, padding
and steerhide over the ash hames, to haul
sledges of cordwood for drying through spring and summer,
for the Glenwood stove next winter, and for the simmering range.

In April you pulled cartloads of manure to spread on the fields,
dark manure of Holsteins, and knobs of your own clustered with oats.
All summer you mowed the grass in meadow and hayfield, the mowing
     machine
clacketing beside you, while the sun walked high in the morning;

and after noon's heat, you pulled a clawed rake through the same acres,
gathering stacks, and dragged the wagon from stack to stack,
and the built hayrack back, uphill to the chaffy barn,
three loads of hay a day from standing grass in the morning.

Sundays you trotted the two miles to church with the light load
of a leather quartertop buggy, and grazed in the sound of hymns.
Generation on generation, your neck rubbed the windowsill
of the stall, smoothing the wood as the sea smooths glass.

When you were old and lame, when your shoulders hurt bending to graze,
one October the man, who fed you and kept you, and harnessed you
     every morning,
led you through corn stubble to sandy ground above Eagle Pond,
and dug a hole beside you where you stood shuddering in your skin,

and lay the shotgun's muzzle in the boneless hollow behind your ear,
and fired the slug into your brain, and felled you into your grave,
shoveling sand to cover you, setting goldenrod upright above you,
where by next summer a dent in the ground made your monument.

For a hundred and fifty years, in the pasture of dead horses,
 roots of pine trees pushed through the pale curves of your ribs,
yellow blossoms flourished above you in autumn, and in winter
frost heaved your bones in the ground—old toilers, soil makers:

O Roger, Mackerel, Riley, Ned, Nellie, Chester, Lady Ghost.

# Jim Harrison

∎

## WALKING

Walking back on a chill morning past Kilmer's Lake
into the first broad gully, down its trough
and over a ridge of poplar, scrub oak, and into
a larger gully, walking into the slow fresh warmth
of midmorning to Spider Lake where I drank
at a small spring remembered from ten years back;
walking northwest two miles where another gully
opened, seeing a stump on a knoll where my father
stood one deer season, and tiring of sleet and cold
burned a pine stump, the snow gathering fire-orange
on a dull day; walking past charred stumps blackened
by the '81 fire to a great hollow stump near a basswood
swale—I sat within it on a November morning
watching deer browse beyond my young range of shotgun
and slug, chest beating hard for killing—
into the edge of a swale waist high with ferns,
seeing the quick movement of a blue racer,
and thick curl of the snake against a birch log,
a pale blue with nothing of the sky in it,
a fleshy blue, blue of knotted veins in an arm;
walking to Savage's Lake where I ate my bread
and cheese, drank cool lake water, and slept for a while,
dreaming of fire, snake and fish and women in white
linen walking, pinkish warm limbs beneath white linen;
then waking, walking homeward toward Well's Lake,
brain at boil now with heat, afternoon glistening
in yellow heat, dead dun-brown grass, windless,
with all distant things shimmering, grasshoppers, birds
dulled to quietness; walking a log road near a cedar swamp
looking cool with green darkness and whine of mosquitoes,
crow's caw overhead, Cooper's hawk floating singly
in mateless haze; walking dumbly, footsore, cutting
into evening through sumac and blackberry brambles,
onto the lake road, feet sliding in the gravel,
whippoorwills, night birds wakening, stumbling to lake
shore, shedding clothes on sweet moss; walking
into syrupy August moonless dark, water cold, pushing
lily pads aside, walking out into the lake with feet
springing on mucky bottom until the water flows overhead;
sinking again to walk on the bottom then buoyed up,
walking on the surface, moving through beds of reeds,
snakes and frogs moving, to the far edge of the lake
then walking upward over the basswood and alders, the field
of sharp stubble and hay bales, toward the woods,

floating over the bushy crests of hardwoods and tips
of pine, barely touching in miles of rolling heavy dark,
coming to the larger water, there walking along the troughs
of waves folding in upon themselves; walking to an island,
small, narrow, sandy, sparsely wooded, in the middle
of the island in a clump of cedars a small spring
which I enter, sliding far down into a deep cool
dark endless weight of water.


## POEM

Form is the woods: the beast,
a bobcat padding through red sumac,
the pheasant in brake or goldenrod
that he stalks—both rise to the flush,
the brief low flutter and catch in air;
and trees, rich green, the moving of boughs
and the separate leaf, yield
to conclusions they do not care about
or watch—the dead, frayed bird,
the beautiful plumage,
the spoor of feathers
and slight, pink bones.

# Robert Hass

∎

## SPRING RAIN

Now the rain is falling, freshly, in the intervals between sunlight,

a Pacific squall started no one knows where, drawn east
as the drifts of warm air make a channel;

it moves its own way, like water or the mind,

and spills this rain passing over. The Sierras will catch
it as last snow flurries before summer, observed only by
the wakened marmots at ten thousand feet,

and we will come across it again as larkspur and penstemon
sprouting along a creek above Sonora Pass next August,

where the snowmelt will have trickled into Dead Man's Creek and
the creek spilled into the Stanislaus and the Stanislaus into
the San Joaquin and the San Joaquin into the slow salt marshes
of the bay.

That's not the end of it: the gray jays of the mountains
eat larkspur seeds which cannot propagate otherwise.

To simulate the process you have to soak gathered seeds
all night in the acids of old coffee

and then score them gently with a very sharp knife before
you plant them in the garden.

You might use what was left of the coffee we drank in Lisa's
kitchen visiting.

There were orange poppies on the table in a clear glass vase,
stained near the bottom to the color of sunrise;

the unstated theme was the blessedness of gathering and the
blessing of dispersal—

it made you glad for beauty like that, casual and intense,
lasting as long as the poppies last.

# John Hay

∎

## MUSIC BY THE WATERS

Out of the marbled underwaters,
artifacts of surf, comes the shining
of bubble and frog-green weed; the salivated
quartz egg; purple dye of greater storms
in minor shells; all things touched by tides;
patterns of water not of water;
castoffs, like speckled eyes from deeper sight,
tones on the mind. I pick them and they sing.


## COMB JELLY

But for the eight, interior rays,
this might be a dislocated eye,
the vitreous humor, horrifying
on the sand. It is nine tenths water,
the sea's ally, and it devours
larvae like a pulsing flower,
a delicate, diaphanous engineering
with magic in its appetite.
One more of Hunger's masterpieces
to make us swallow what we see.

# Anthony Hecht

∎

## A HILL

In Italy, where this sort of thing can occur,
I had a vision once—though you understand
It was nothing at all like Dante's, or the visions of saints,
And perhaps not a vision at all. I was with some friends,
Picking my way through a warm sunlit piazza
In the early morning. A clear fretwork of shadows
From huge umbrellas littered the pavement and made
A sort of lucent shallows in which was moored
A small navy of carts. Books, coins, old maps,
Cheap landscapes and ugly religious prints
Were all on sale. The colors and noise
Like the flying hands were gestures of exultation,
So that even the bargaining
Rose to the ear like a voluble godliness.
And then, when it happened, the noises suddenly stopped,
And it got darker; pushcarts and people dissolved
And even the great Farnese Palace itself
Was gone, for all its marble; in its place
Was a hill, mole-colored and bare. It was very cold,
Close to freezing, with a promise of snow.
The trees were like old ironwork gathered for scrap
Outside a factory wall. There was no wind,
And the only sound for a while was the little click
Of ice as it broke in the mud under my feet.
I saw a piece of ribbon snagged on a hedge,
But no other sign of life. And then I heard
What seemed the crack of a rifle. A hunter, I guessed;
At least I was not alone. But just after that
Came the soft and papery crash
Of a great branch somewhere unseen falling to earth.

And that was all, except for the cold and silence
That promised to last forever, like the hill.

Then prices came through, and fingers, and I was restored
To the sunlight and my friends. But for more than a week
I was scared by the plain bitterness of what I had seen.
All this happened about ten years ago,
And it hasn't troubled me since, but at last, today,
I remembered that hill; it lies just to the left
Of the road north of Poughkeepsie; and as a boy
I stood before it for hours in wintertime.

# William Heyen

∎

## THE HOST

In the dying pond,
under an oilspilled rainbow where
cement clumped, cans rusted, and slick tires
glinted their whitewall irises,
at the edge where liquid congealed,
a lump of mud shifted.
I knew what it was,
and knelt to poke it with a wire
from the saddest mattress in the world.

Maybe a month out of its rubbery egg,
the young snapper hid,
or tried to, drew back its head,
but algae-scum outlined its oval shell,
its ridged chine diminished
toward its tail,
and I lifted the turtle
into the air, its jaws open,
its crooked neck unfolding upward.

It twisted, could not reach me.
I found out its soft, small undershell where,
already, a leech lodged
beneath its left hindleg, sucking
some of whatever blood
its host could filter from the pond, its host.
They would grow together, if the snapper lived.
Its yellow eyes insisted it would.
I gave it back to the oil sludge

where it was born, and watched it
bury itself, in time, and disappear. . . .
I'd like to leave it living there,
but churned slime above its blurs, burns,
bursts into black glare, every atom
of chemical water, rust residue, human vomit
shining in deathlight.
The snapper's bleached shell ascends the 21st century,
empty, beyond illusion.

# Linda Hogan

∎

## ELK SONG

We give thanks
to deer, otter,
the great fish
and birds that fly over
and are our bones and skin.
Even the yelping dog at our heels
is a hungry crow
picking bones wolf left behind.
And thanks to the corn and trees.
The earth
is a rich table
and a slaughterhouse
for humans as well.

But this is for the elk,
the red running one
like thunder over hills,
a saint with its holy hoof dance
an old woman whose night song
we try not to hear.

This song is for the elk
with its throat whistling
and antlers
above head and great hooves
rattling earth.

One spring night, elk
ran across me
while I slept on earth
and every hoof missed
my shaking bones.

That other time, I heard elk run
on earth's tight skin,
the time I was an enemy
from the other side of the forest.
Didn't I say the earth is a slaughterhouse
for humans as well?

Some nights in town's cold winter,
earth shakes.
People say it's a train full of danger
or the plane-broken barriers of sound,
but out there
behind the dark trunks of trees
the gone elk have pulled the hide of earth
tight and they are drumming
back the woodland,
tall grass and days we were equal
and strong.

## THE AVALANCHE

Just last month
the avalanches like good women
were headed for a downfall. I saw one
throw back her head
and let go of the world.

No more free soup bones for that one.
No more faces of friends at the door
with doilies and lace,
with ivory charms
carved of the elephant's great collapse.

Once an avalanche makes up her mind
not to cling,
there's no more covering up the cliff face
and hiding the truth,
and in her breakdown
she knows everything
and knows what she knows
about the turning wheel of earth,
love, markets, and even the spring
coming soon with its wildflowers.

# Janet Holmes

∎

## PASTORAL

I don't know much about sheep, don't know
how big they can get or how smart they are, why
they seem to come only in black and white, or how to read
the red patches of ownership blazed on their backs.
In Sligo and Donegal they crowded the car
off the road on nearly every road we drove,
with sometimes a dog or small boy chasing,
a constant glottal chatter rising from the herd.
Sheep really *do* say "baa"; they hold the breaking word
in their throats until it crumbles. It was May,
some of the lambs made their first clumsy runs
avoiding us. And hiking Slieve League
or down near Drumcliff, we found them:
guarding high crosses and dolmens, grazing
the mound where a witch was buried, wandering
down to the tiny strands from their western hills;
we saw them in roofless ruins too minor
to be named in guidebooks. And, on a small road,
found a diamond-shaped yellow sign with three
white sheep—a handmade "sheep crossing"
that made you laugh. When you did, I remembered
the long time it had been since I'd said
I loved you, and said it. For once
I picked a good moment: spring,
our first long time alone, and a scene
set up for lovers back in the sixteenth century.
It would have been natural for that time to be perfect—
perfect!—the definition of romance. Looking back, though,
I remember the blank faces of sheep
perhaps more than I should, see their dark ears
flapping as they feed, their grave
stupid bodies; I hear their noise.

# David Huddle

■

## THE NATURE OF YEARNING
*for Lindsey and Elizabeth*

I

This northern August swells with warmth
the garden would burst and a trout waits
beneath the moving river surface
he holds steady until the brown caddis
fly floats above him he plunges upward
breaks the silent water then slaps down fat
as deer that graze the flat meadows while slowly
as in a dream of shadows a black bear circles
beneath trees ten thousand shades of green.

II

All changed now quickened the morning
air in September lifts the spirit high
as one perfect trumpet note still
this clarity this concerto suggests
the coming death of tomato vines also
cucumber broccoli corn beans peas yellow
squash cauliflower all vegetables dead
or dying we wait the swelling of pumpkins
the blood flame turning of delicate leaves.

III

High down out of Canada the geese were flying
all day my wife said that far-off honking
sound makes you feel lonely the trees were pure
fire for two weeks but now the leaves have fallen
all purple and brown the woods resound with axes
while men cut logs the children home from school
go out for kindling the leaves crackle the blood
of the animals flows richer and a white-tail doe
sniffs the air at dusk her smoky fawn now half-grown.

IV

Chop the caught turkey's neck catch the buck
deer in gunsights fire shots deep into his heart
sling up his carcass to a thick tree cut open
his belly and handle the bloody heat and stink
of his guts shoot doves partridge quail
pheasant and grouse shoot rabbits shoot quick
squirrels and walk the stubbled fields with meat
on your back for soon the snow comes and with it
the silence at night when the wind wants man flesh.

V

White December the elegance of pine trees
in snow with voices risen in praise of Christ
the soft child of winter all Bach Fasch
and Handel cannot hold Jesus' swelling song
but now the trout takes no food the bass
sinks into the darkest pools of the river
the bear's blood slows while goose and duck
have long flown south and beside the house
snow deepens over logs stacked for the fire.

VI

Ice ice the death of trees the wind strips them bare
it whips them into savage rooted dances branches
crack limbs are yanked off they fall and smatter
on the frozen ground fearing wind I tell my wife
don't stand by that window a pane might burst
this morning she found stiff on the crusty ice
a redpoll dead and light as dust in her hand she said
the sun has forgotten us the nights go on and on
the clouds flee and the wind howls all day long.

VII

No meat in the house we cut holes in the ice
this February we fished for smelt and perch the ice
on the lake was two feet thick my wife thinks
the birds have left us forever only the rats thrive
they steal our corn and leave us just cobs and husks
rabbits are hard to track now but one the other day
sat in the field he was so cold I walked up and kicked
him before I shot the ice builds its kingdom
and holds against what fire we have left love.

## VIII

We long for warmth these days there is little sun
still no birds have flown north over our house
and I think this March no month for birth only
the wind has life no green anywhere the trees
are just bones they shiver and bend they want
loose from this earth yesterday we saw the grass
it was brown and dead as an old hide in daylight
the snow melts some but it freezes again at night
the ground is covered with brittle crusts of thin ice.

## IX

Oh the waters burst there are the timid green buds
delicate grass crocus and daffodil the waters
gather they flow out of the mountain the streams
wash off dead limbs and leaves the gentle rains
bring birth this air of April wakes even the animals
the spring birds have come back the trout leaps again
now the wind is a child the earth is sunlit a woman
walks outside this morning she is beautiful as the clear
sweet sound a man makes with his horn at his lips.

# Andrew Hudgins

∎

## THE PERSISTENCE OF NATURE IN OUR LIVES

You find them in the darker woods
occasionally—those swollen lumps
of fungus, twisted, moist, and yellow—
but when they show up on the lawn
it's like they've tracked me home. In spring
the persistence of nature in our lives
rises from below, drifts from above.
The pollen settles on my skin
and waits for me to bloom, trying
to work green magic on my flesh.
They're indiscriminate, these firs.
They'll mate with anything. A great
green-yellow cloud of pollen sifts
across the house. The waste of it
leaves nothing out—not even men.
The pollen doesn't care I'm not
a tree. The golden storm descends.
Wind lifts it from the branches, lofts
it in descending arches of need
and search, a grainy yellow haze
that settles over everything
as if it's all the same. I love
the utter waste of pollen, a scum
of it on every pond and puddle.
It rides the ripples and, when they dry,
remains, a line of yellow dust
zigzagging in the shape of waves.
One night, perhaps a little drunk,
I stretched out on the porch, watching
the Milky Way. At dawn I woke
to find a man-shape on the hard
wood floor, outlined in pollen—a sharp
spread-eagle figure drawn there like
the body at a murder scene.
Except for that spot, the whole damn house
glittered, green-gold. I wandered out
across the lawn, my bare feet damp
with dew, the wet ground soft, forgiving,
beneath my step. I understood
I am, as much as anyone,
the golden beast who staggers home,
in June, beneath the yearning trees.

# Laura Jensen

∎

## LANDSCAPE

Nothing can oppose the cloud.
Nothing can oppose the gray
that sponges up the rust
off the old grass,
unless it is the stone
of its own color
in the tower
where the windows webbed over
are less open than its padlocked door.

It is not the gray birds
it is not the talons of birds
it is not the weather
or the trees that play dead
or the gray eyes of an old woman
or the children who are watching the ground
for sticks.

See what is coming—
a landscape where we take in turn
what is bleak and empty.
You do not comprehend yourself
until someone steps to you,
grateful you are carrying that lantern.

# Richard Kenney

∎

## THE EVOLUTION OF THE FLIGHTLESS BIRD

*The First Poem in Twelve Months*

awkward as evolution of flight itself taxis
in the bushveldt, paddles twitching, recalling carrion
from a thousand feet, and oh, the eyes, cobalt
ice and flashing in a field of green—Careening
now, lips back, legs drive, *flap, flap,* bald
flippers slap his sides—to lift, to climb uncobbled
air, to leave his tracks. . . . But green earth still attracts
him, heavy, still, except his eyes, which feather hope
as a green point describes an arc across
a blank oscilloscope: *escape,* escape
velocity: this is the language of desire
itself, the high skywritten screech of genus *Icarus,*
whose frayed sleeves snap and leap like parting cables,
quills across his foolscap, barbed lines thick with *cire*


*Perdue*

and downy wool. . . . Not lost, if lost among the limbs
and stems still trembling from his passage, shallow orbit
like a feathered cannonball, a swept-winged boar-
let-off-a-bowstring six and eight feet at a bound—
Catch sight of him—again, and gone—a glimpse. . . .
We'll trace him, follow fossil footprints past the turnstile
where the Royal Garden's glass house is. Arboreal
mosses torn and swaying, stripped lianas ribboned
out behind him, crushed shoots, ferns and forest orchids
crushed, spore cases flat—note newly pollinated
flowers in a cloud of dust, where broken plants
seep milky sap, a sweet wind stirs the stale
cloud-chamber here, and ground speed is a perfect arc
in two dimensions, following the planet's


*Fall Line*

down—Now follow down into the dense
frond-choked chambers where the story finds its source:
this is the Orphic epic of the Age: imagine
names, time out of mind, *Phororhacos,*
or *Diatryma.* . . . Lacewings thin as oxygen

catch light where dragonflies a foot across
whirr overhead at dusk; and flying foxes,
huge fruit-eating bats, still swoop the garden's
glass walls, echoing; and see, too, pterosaurs
whose mucid wings will fold us in like eyelids,
like dream. . . . We'll cup bird calls as frail as matchlight
in our palms, and roll out fruit, and mix exotic
nectars with the dew at dawn, to try
to draw them back, attract them, *Diatryma*


## *Phororhacos*

Horse-high carnivores bestride our dreams, their crescent
beaks curved down like the horned moon—Vanished, past
masters of the Miocene savannahs, eyes
as blue as heaven still, as still as resins
where all wings are trapped in mind. . . . Where great birds,
unbridled, saurian, renowned for their rapacity
in middle earth once raced the flat limestone horizons
underfoot, when air speed slipped on ground speed, shrieking
like asbestos burned away to nothing, to air—then burst
all bounds, bones elongate, light, antique
and delicate and wheeling, wheeling in the windy city
of the birds again. . . . Observe, though, thin shellacs
of ice begin to form, to glaze their wings—they rise,
slip sideways, slide like flat cards toward the shell-like


## *Earth*

blue robin's egg a thousand feet below—The first
poem in twelve months faint and losing ground grinds
its passage through the stacked-stone glass-house strata
lit with history and hell's and heaven's flint-
to-tinder, tracing out the pyrotechnic line
to earth again. This is the story of the fierce
heart netted by the paralytic hand, in time,
in mind, a row of bamboo cages burst behind. . . .
Just so, these cubicles. Inside, a lint
like eiderdown, a pinfeather or two, birdlime,
the air astir—and loose bars hollow as a syrinx
whistling with it still, where the snake-necked ratite
genie of the thing's escaped, as all *errata*
do, in cursive gyres, high rings, high rings—

# Galway Kinnell

∎

## THE PORCUPINE

### 1

Fatted
on herbs, swollen on crabapples,
puffed up on bast and phloem, ballooned
on willow flowers, poplar catkins, first
leafs of aspen and larch,
the porcupine
drags and bounces his last meal through ice,
mud, roses and goldenrod, into the stubbly high fields.

### 2

In character
he resembles us in seven ways:
he puts his mark on outhouses,
he alchemizes by moonlight,
he shits on the run,
he uses his tail for climbing,
he chuckles softly to himself when scared,
he's overcrowded if there's more than one of him per five acres,
his eyes have their own inner redness.

### 3

Digger of
goings across floors, of hesitations
at thresholds, of
handprints of dread
at doorpost or window jamb, he would
gouge the world
empty of us, hack and crater
it
until it is nothing, if that
could rid it of all our sweat and pathos.

Adorer of axe
handles aflow with grain, of arms
of Morris chairs, of hand
crafted objects
steeped in the juice of fingertips,
of surfaces wetted down
with fist grease and elbow oil,
of clothespins that have
grabbed our body-rags by underarm and crotch . . .

Unimpressed—bored—
by the whirl of the stars, by *these*
he's astonished, ultra-
Rilkean angel!

for whom the true
portion of the sweetness of earth
is one of those bottom-heavy, glittering, saccadic
bits
of salt water that splash down
the haunted ravines of a human face.

4

A farmer shot a porcupine three times
as it dozed on a tree limb. On
the way down it tore open its belly
on a broken
branch, hooked its gut,
and went on falling. On the ground
it sprang to its feet, and
paying out gut heaved
and spartled through a hundred feet of goldenrod
before
the abrupt emptiness.

5

The Avesta
puts porcupine killers
into hell for nine generations, sentencing them
to gnaw out
each other's hearts for the
salts of desire.

I roll
this way and that in the great bed, under
the quilt
that mimics this country of broken farms and woods,
the fatty sheath of the man
melting off,
the self-stabbing coil
of bristles reversing, blossoming outward—
a red-eyed, hard-toothed, arrow-struck urchin
tossing up mattress feathers,
pricking the
woman beside me until she cries.

6

In my time I have
crouched, quills erected,
Saint
Sebastian of the
scared heart, and been
beat dead with a locust club
on the bare snout.
And fallen from high places
I have fled, have
jogged
over fields of goldenrod,
terrified, seeking home,
and among flowers
I have come to myself empty, the rope
strung out behind me
in the fall sun
suddenly glorified with all my blood.

7

And tonight I think I prowl broken
skulled or vacant as a
sucked egg in the wintry meadow, softly chuckling, blank
template of myself, dragging
a starved belly through the lichflowered acres,
where
burdock looses the ark of its seed
and thistle holds up its lost bloom
and rosebushes in the wind scrape their dead limbs
for the forced-fire
of roses.

## DAYBREAK

On the tidal mud, just before sunset,
dozens of starfishes
were creeping. It was
as though the mud were a sky
and enormous, imperfect stars
moved across it as slowly
as the actual stars cross heaven.
All at once they stopped,
and as if they had simply
increased their receptivity
to gravity they sank down
into the mud; they faded down
into it and lay still; and by the time
pink of sunset broke across them
they were as invisible
as the true stars at daybreak.

## BLACKBERRY EATING

I love to go out in late September
among the fat, overripe, icy, black blackberries
to eat blackberries for breakfast,
the stalks very prickly, a penalty
they earn for knowing the black art
of blackberry-making; and as I stand among them
lifting the stalks to my mouth, the ripest berries
fall almost unbidden to my tongue,
as words sometimes do, certain peculiar words
like *strengths* or *squinched*,
many-lettered, one-syllabled lumps,
which I squeeze, squinch open, and splurge well
in the silent, startled, icy, black language
of blackberry-eating in late September.

# Ted Kooser

∎

## PORCH SWING IN SEPTEMBER

The porch swing hangs fixed in a morning sun
that bleaches its gray slats, its flowered cushion
whose flowers have faded, like those of summer,
and a small brown spider has hung out her web
on a line between porch post and chain
so that no one may swing without breaking it.
She is saying it's time that the swinging were done with,
time that the creaking and pinging and popping
that sang through the ceiling were past,
time now for the soft vibrations of moths,
the wasp tapping each board for an entrance,
the cool dewdrops to brush from her work
every morning, one world at a time.

## A BUFFALO SKULL

No fine white bone-sheen now;
a hundred hard years
have worn it away, this stump
washed up on a bar
in the river, its horns
like broken roots,
its muzzle filled with sand
and the thin gray breath
of spider webs. Once,
they covered the grasslands
like the shadows of clouds,
and now the river gives up
just one skull, a hive of bone
like a fallen wasp's nest,
heavy, empty, and
full of the whine of the wind
and old thunder.

# Maxine Kumin

∎

## HOW IT GOES ON

Today I trade my last unwise
ewe lamb, the one who won't leave home,
for two cords of stove-length oak
and wait on the old enclosed
front porch to make the swap.
November sun revives the thick
trapped buzz of horseflies. The siren
for noon and forest fires blows
a sliding scale. The lamb of woe
looks in at me through glass
on the last day of her life.

Geranium scraps from the window box
trail from her mouth, burdock burrs
are stickered to her fleece like chicken pox,
under her tail stub, permanent smears.

I think of how it goes on,
this dark particular bent of our hungers:
the way wire eats into a tree
year after year on the pasture's perimeter,
keeping the milk cows penned
until they grow too old to freshen;
of how the last wild horses were scoured
from canyons in Idaho, roped, thrown,
their nostrils twisted shut with wire
to keep them down, the mares aborting,
days later, all of them carted to town.

I think of how it will be
in January, nights so cold
the pond ice cracks like target practice,
daylight glue-colored, sleet falling,
my yellow horse slick with the ball-bearing
sleet, raising up from his dingy browse
out of boredom and habit
to strip bark from the fenced-in trees;
of February, month of the hard palate,
the split wood running out,
worms working in the flour bin.

The lamb, whose time has come, goes off
in the cab of the dump truck, tied to the seat
with baling twine, durable enough
to bear her to the knife and rafter.

O lambs! The whole wolf-world sits down to eat
and cleans its muzzle after.

# Stanley Kunitz

∎

## THE SNAKES OF SEPTEMBER

All summer I heard them
rustling in the shrubbery,
outracing me from tier
to tier in my garden,
a whisper among the viburnums,
a signal flashed from the hedgerow,
a shadow pulsing
in the barberry thicket.
Now that the nights are chill
and the annuals spent,
I should have thought them gone,
in a torpor of blood
slipped to the nether world
before the sickle frost.
Not so. In the deceptive balm
of noon, as if defiant of the curse
that spoiled another garden,
these two appear on show
through a narrow slit
in the dense green brocade
of a north-country spruce,
dangling head-down, entwined
in a brazen love-knot.
I put out my hand and stroke
the fine, dry grit of their skins.
After all,
we are partners in this land,
co-signers of a covenant.
At my touch the wild
braid of creation
trembles.

# The Wellfleet Whale

*A few summers ago, on Cape Cod, a whale foundered on the beach, a sixty-three-foot finback whale. When the tide went out, I approached him. He was lying there, in monstrous desolation, making the most terrifying noises—rumbling—groaning. I put my hands on his flanks and I could feel the life inside him. And while I was standing there, suddenly he opened his eye. It was a big, red, cold eye, and it was staring directly at me. A shudder of recognition passed between us. Then the eye closed forever. I've been thinking about whales ever since.*

*—Journal entry*

1

You have your language too,
    an eerie medley of clicks
        and hoots and trills,
location-notes and love calls,
    whistles and grunts. Occasionally,
        it's like furniture being smashed,
or the creaking of a mossy door,
    sounds that all melt into a liquid
        song with endless variations,
as if to compensate
    for the vast loneliness of the sea.
        Sometimes a disembodied voice
breaks in, as if from distant reefs,
    and it's as much as one can bear
        to listen to its long mournful cry,
a sorrow without name, both more
    and less than human. It drags
        across the ear like a record
running down.

2

No wind. No waves. No clouds.
    Only the whisper of the tide,
        as it withdrew, stroking the shore,
a lazy drift of gulls overhead,
    and tiny points of light
        bubbling in the channel.
It was the tag-end of summer.
    From the harbor's mouth
        you coasted into sight,
flashing news of your advent,
    the crescent of your dorsal fin
        clipping the diamonded surface.
We cheered at the sign of your greatness
    when the black barrel of your head
        erupted, ramming the water,

93

and you flowered for us
in the jet of your spouting.


3

All afternoon you swam
tirelessly round the bay,
with such an easy motion,
the slightest downbeat of your tail,
an almost imperceptible
undulation of your flippers,
you seemed like something poured,
not driven; you seemed
to marry grace with power.
And when you bounded into air,
slapping your flukes,
we thrilled to look upon
pure energy incarnate
as nobility of form.
You seemed to ask of us
not sympathy, or love,
or understanding,
but awe and wonder.

That night we watched you
swimming in the moon.
Your back was molten silver.
We guessed your silent passage
by the phosphorescence in your wake.
At dawn we found you stranded on the rocks.


4

There came a boy and a man
and yet other men running, and two
schoolgirls in yellow halters
and a housewife bedecked
with curlers, and whole families in beach
buggies with assorted yelping dogs.
The tide was almost out.
We could walk around you,
as you heaved deeper into the shoal,
crushed by your own weight,
collapsing into yourself,
your flippers and your flukes
quivering, your blowhole
spasmodically bubbling, roaring.
In the pit of your gaping mouth
you bared your fringework of baleen,
a thicket of horned bristles.
When the Curator of Mammals

arrived from Boston
    to take samples of your blood
        you were already oozing from below.
Somebody had carved his initials
    in your flank. Hunters of souvenirs
        had peeled off strips of your skin,
a membrane thin as paper.
    You were blistered and cracked by the sun.
        The gulls had been pecking at you.
The sound you made was a hoarse and fitful bleating.

What drew us, like a magnet, to your dying?
    You made a bond between us,
        the keepers of the nightfall watch,
who gathered in a ring around you,
    boozing in the bonfire light.
        Toward dawn we shared with you
your hour of desolation,
    the huge lingering passion
        of your unearthly outcry,
as you swung your blind head
    toward us and laboriously opened
        a bloodshot, glistening eye,
in which we swam with terror and recognition.

5

Voyager, chief of the pelagic world,
    you brought with you the myth
        of another country, dimly remembered,
where flying reptiles
    lumbered over the steaming marshes
        and trumpeting thunder lizards
wallowed in the reeds.
    While empires rose and fell on land,
        your nation breasted the open main,
rocked in the consoling rhythm
    of the tides. Which ancestor first plunged
        head-down through zones of colored twilight
to scour the bottom of the dark?
    You ranged the North Atlantic track
        from Port-of-Spain to Baffin Bay,
edging between the ice-floes
    through the fat of summer,
        lob-tailing, breaching, sounding,
grazing in the pastures of the sea
    on krill-rich orange plankton
        crackling with life.
You prowled down the continental shelf,
    guided by the sun and stars
        and the taste of alluvial silt

on your way southward
    to the warm lagoons,
        the tropic of desire,
where the lovers lie belly to belly
    in the rub and nuzzle of their sporting;
        and you turned, like a god in exile,
out of your wide primeval element,
    delivered to the mercy of time.
        Master of the whale-roads,
let the white wings of the gulls
    spread out their cover.
        You have become like us,
disgraced and mortal.

# Denise Levertov

∎

## THE GROUND-MIST

In hollows of the land
in faults and valleys
                    the white fog
bruised
          by blue shadows
a mirage of lakes

and in the human
faults and depths
                    silences
floating
          between night and daybreak
illusion and substance.

But is illusion
so repeated, known
                    each dawn,
silence
      suspended in the
mind's shadow

always, not substance
of a sort?
          the white
bruised
          ground-mist the mirage
of a true lake.

## O TASTE AND SEE

The world is
not with us enough.
**O taste and see**

the subway Bible poster said,
meaning **The Lord,** meaning
if anything all that lives
to the imagination's tongue,

grief, mercy, language,
tangerine, weather, to
breathe them, bite,
savor, chew, swallow, transform

into our flesh our
deaths, crossing the street, plum, quince,
living in the orchard and being

hungry, and plucking
the fruit.


## COME INTO ANIMAL PRESENCE

Come into animal presence.
No man is so guileless as
the serpent. The lonely white
rabbit on the roof is a star
twitching its ears at the rain.
The llama intricately
folding its hind legs to be seated
not disdains but mildly
disregards human approval.
What joy when the insouciant
armadillo glances at us and doesn't
quicken his trotting
across the track into the palm brush.

What is this joy? That no animal
falters, but knows what it must do?
That the snake has no blemish,
that the rabbit inspects his strange surroundings
in white star-silence? The llama
rests in dignity, the armadillo
has some intention to pursue in the palm-forest.
Those who were sacred have remained so,
holiness does not dissolve, it is a presence
of bronze, only the sight that saw it
faltered and turned from it.
An old joy returns in holy presence.

# Philip Levine

∎

## To a Fish Head Found on the Beach Near Malaga

### I

Flat, eventless afternoon
searching among the stones for nothing
I come upon the fish head.
                              "¡Hola!"
Right off, head to head, with this
wide-eyed, unlistening remnant
of dead metal trailing its single
stiff feather of flesh.
                        We talk of loneliness,
of the fear of stones falling like rain,
hatred of water tumbling out of dreams
and filling our small rooms. Shafts of sand
sifting under doors, filming
first the glasses, then the eyes,
weighing down the lips, the cry.

### II

                        Here, halfway
from home, I discover my head, its hideous
King Tongue going. My good hands explore it,
the hair thinning, the eyes scratched
and hot, that let the lids thump down,
and the poor muscles, unsleeping,
as burned as drawn ropes.
Only the chin happy, hidden in fur.

### III

But how good to find companionship
of any kind. Fish head and man head,
communing in their tongue, an iron yawn
out over the waves, the one poem born
of the eternal and always going back.
I throw the fish head to the sea.
Let it be fish once more.
                          I sniff my fingers
and catch the burned essential oil
seeping out of death. Out of beginning,
I hear, under the sea roar, the bone words
of teeth tearing earth and sea,
anointing the tongues with stone and sand,
water eating fish, fish water,
head eating head to let us be.

# Thomas McGrath

∎

## PRAISES

The vegetables please us with their modes and virtues.
                                        The demure heart
Of the lettuce inside its circular court, baroque ear
Of quiet under its rustling house of lace, pleases
Us.
      And the bold strength of the celery, its green Hispanic
¡Shout! its exclamatory confetti.
                                And the analogue that is Onion:
Ptolemaic astronomy and tearful allegory, the Platonic circles
Of His inexhaustible soul!
                                O and the straightforwardness
In the labyrinth of Cabbage, the infallible rectitude of Homegrown
      Mushroom
Under its cone of silence like a papal hat—
                                        All these
Please us.
            And the syllabus of the corn,
                                that wampum,
                                        its golden
Roads leading out of the wigwams of its silky and youthful smoke;
The nobility of the dill, cool in its silences and cathedrals;
Tomatoes five-alarm fires in their musky barrios, peas
Asleep in their cartridge clips,
                                beetsblood,
                                        colonies of the imperial
Cauliflower, and the buddha-like seeds of the pepper
Turning their prayerwheels in the green gloom of their caves.
All these we praise: they please us all ways: these smallest virtues.
All these earth-given:
                        and the heaven-hung fruit also . . .
                                        As instance
Banana which continually makes angelic ears out of sour
Purses, or the winy abacus of the holy grape on its cross
Of alcohol, or the peach with its fur like a young girl's—
All these we praise: the winter in the flesh of the apple, and the sun
Domesticated under the orange's rind.
                                We praise
By the skin of our teeth, Persimmon, and Pawpaw's constant
Affair with gravity, and the proletariat of the pomegranate
Inside its leathery city.
                        And let us praise all these
As they please us: skin, flesh, flower, and the flowering
Bones of their seeds: from which come orchards: bees: honey:
Flowers, love's language, love, heart's ease, poems, praise.

# THE RETURN

The trees are never the same
                    twice
                        the animals
                                the birds or
The little river lying on its back in the sun or the sun or
The varying moon changing over the changing hills
Constant.
            It is this, still, that most I love about them.

I enter by dark or day:
                    that green noise, dying
Alive and living its death, that inhuman circular singing,
May call me stranger . . .
                    Or the little doors of the bark open
And I enter that other home outside the tent of my skin . . .

On such days, on such midnights, I have gone, I will go,
Past the human, past the animal, past the bird,
To the old mothers who stand with their feet in the loamy dark
And their green and gold praises playing into the sun . . .

For a little while, only. (It is a long way back.)
But at least, and if but for a moment, I have almost entered the stone.
Then fear and love call. I am cast out. Alien,
On the bridge of fur and of feather I go back to the world I have known.


# HISTORY

All night the wind
Yelled at the house,
The trees squeaked and hushed
But the wind would not.
All night the trees complained
And the rain rushed and rained.

Now in the cool
Morning the trees stand, tall,
Still and all composed—
Sun on their sunny pages.
Of the storm only the riled
Creek remembers; and rages.

# Heather McHugh

∎

## THE FIELD

It was my day to study
in the field. I found
fences strung with glass beads,
small possessions of shock,
the farms of his and hers.
I couldn't make myself at home.
I lowed so the cow would
but the cow looked up, misquoted.
When I got back to the house
my five hired fellow-specialists
were taping their abstracts
to the window. Soon it would be dark.

## ELEMENTAL

I want to last one more winter,
live in this austerity and learn
the elements responsible
for weeping, burning,
burying and song.

I want to hear the hours
of vibration in a glass of ice,
see the blues in the five-sided fire.
You aim your gun at the trembling
hill, and want the world to break

from cover. I say only
raise your hand against the sun,
darken my hair instead. Enter
into love as bare necessity;
the blueberry will turn ten acres red.

# Lynne McMahon

∎

## IN THE GARDEN

1 / Earth

They are incontrovertible, the evidences
Of spring. How completely the robin clears
The lip of the feeder and ground beneath.
How intent the cat is, advancing on the mole
Over the invisible grubs that feed it
In the dark excavations. Pushing
The lawn mower over a yard gone spongy with
Tunnels, you think only fleetingly
Of the first salt sweating down your back
Like the mysteries of origin, while your gloves,
Braced against the shudder of grips, curl
And hold fast, guiding you past the tall trees
Which are the demarcations of Paradise.

2 / I Know Two Birds

The swallow, but only in flight,
        And the male cardinal.
Oh, I'm right about the blue jay
        And pigeon, of course,
But in the aviary of timeless
        Splendor
They are the commoners,
        As I am,
Visitor,
        Dragging the ferrule of
My umbrella past
        Students with their sketchpads
Encamped here because the daylight
        Lasts past nine.

So I can't describe these
        Beyond the brown
Uniform
        Sometimes broken by
Yellow bars
        Or eye rings,
But the song, the song
        Goes on revolving

In the deepening bowl of the sky.
        It undresses the earth
For the bath, holds out
        The thick uncurtained moonlight
Laying down its wing
        To lay me down to sleep


## 3 / Toward Eve

Up the cement steps and cracked
Sidewalk with its hairline of grass, up
The wood ramp to the porch which is
Beginning a slow sag and rotting
Just perceptibly in the crosshatch
Of latched sticks on the underside,
Off in the shadiest corner contracted
Against the light—this
Is where you kneel. This is the first
Morning after the sea's departure,
After the fish spines adding their nitrogen
To the loam, after the plankton.
In tiny knuckles of upturning life,
The ferns push up into their brains,
Pushing, straightening, finally one morning
(In the thousand hours of the first
Morning) no longer the green sea horses
Of infant plants. They are astride
The earth now, tall
In their first arrogance. The book
Doesn't say how soon they will bend
To the soil and the hidden nocturnal
Creatures beneath. On that, the book
Is silent, as the ferns are, as the woman
Is who stoops to direct their waters, tending
And blending in, as on the sixth day.


## 4 / Empire

    And there were, in the garden,
Dutch iris, beautifully
        Ugly,
The purple underlip
    (Which the grower's guide
Calls a beard)
        Sun-drugged, dragged
Earthward
    So the corolla might rise
Like a wand, producing

The fretwork
Of sun motes and water
   In a presto of light.
Imperious
      Cared-for,
Sown in cold frames or protected
   Seedbeds and left
To sojourn beneath
      The indoor lights—
A nursling slip
   Gardening the skies.
Roses bloomed
      Above the jungle—
But that was years ago.
   Cluster carriers opened
Their calyx
      And petals fell,
Years ago.
   From heaven, the Western World
Is a purple / blue on the map.
      Such a proud flower
Fretting the sun
   To water, water to the grid
That was the earth.

# Sandra McPherson

∎

## MESEMBRYANTHEMUM AND ZAUSCHNERIA

*(Palo Alto Baylands and Monte Bello Open Space Preserve)*

Jewels start seedy. They must crouch underfoot.
Because the rich aren't miners,
full-grown gems have an earthless style
when cleaned and heightened to a neck
or a crown. Down in the sea-winded marsh,
we kneel like lottery winners—
maybe these *are* cheap,
succulents of oozing glass,
not crystal, not silver, not ruby
but wet, seasonal facsimile.
They look like a fortune.
It is poverty, plain, to go see them
so invested in this rubbery property.

At the crossroads in the dry,
oaten, fault-ridden hills,
with most of the wildflowers driven
to seed: hummingbird trumpets,
opened like a box of ornaments.
The dust hasn't dulled them;
they lean upridge as a brush-fire would.
Thatch dies and falls, thin arm
on thin leg, across their red.
We're prompted to go on forever,
but on which poor, footwashing road?
Are we cornered in passions,
ice plant abandoned
for hot-weather, hilly firechalice?
—Or delivered by them?—
The birds drink and start here,
now, to crave the south.

# FRINGECUPS

Of a green so palely, recessively matched to the forest floor,
one asks if they will turn a color
for they could hardly fade more.
Around them, buttercups spread witheringly bright.

But there can be a deep pink sign of aging
on a cup's curled edge.
And when its style calves and the ovary splits,
one drop of cucumber-scented water sprinkles the fingernail.

Here I've found
the exhausted shrew, the kissy snail
in the green steam of a rainstorm.
But wildflowers do the mopping up.

Is it they who define the fringe?
Or the border made by the flooding, reddened creek
one cannot wade or swim across,
one's joy become impassable?

Not that there is anything beyond
this blurring, this infringement of full glory,
but one need, wonderer: you have friends
you are studying for degrees of bliss;

monitor this—how first I became enamored
of these fancy nothings, these teacups so small
tempests can't get in.
It was while walking out of words and into the margin

as into the missed language of a foreign film,
where all I understood was an edginess,
a century unrevisable now, a humor sometimes sexy
and ending in death

like the occasional red lips of one strap of fringecups
in the midst of all the green ones.
By the time anyone might read this
it will be very much too late

for the fringecups' unconfident bells
and yet we will want to keep on
hearing something. They looked
like sound. They led us to believe they could ring.

Where did that strength of illusion come from?
The fringecup evanesced when the weather
turned sunny. Its whole modesty now is gone.
No boasts are in its place.

# William Matthews

## NEW

The long path sap sludges up
through an iris, is it new
each spring? And what would
an iris care for novelty?
Urgent in tatters, it wants
to wrest what routine it can
from the ceaseless shifts
of weather, from the scrounge
it feeds on to grow beautiful
and bigger: last week the space
about to be rumpled
by iris petals was only air
through which a rabbit leapt,
a volley of heartbeats hardly
contained by fur, and then the clay-
colored spaniel in pursuit
and the effortless air
rejoining itself whole.

## CIVILIZATION AND ITS DISCONTENTS

*Integration in, or adaptation to, a human
community appears as a scarcely avoidable
condition which must be fullfilled before
[our] aim of happiness can be achieved.
If it could be done without that condition,
it would perhaps be preferable.*

—Freud

How much of the great poetry
of solitude in the woods is one
long cadenza on the sadness

of civilization, and how much
thought on beaches, between drowsing
and sleep, along the borders,

between one place and another,
as if such poise were home to us?
On the far side of these woods, stew,

gelatinous from cracked lamb shanks,
is being ladled into bowls, and
a family scuffs its chairs close

to an inherited table.
Maybe there's wine, maybe not. We don't
know because our thoughts are with

the great sad soul in the woods again.
We suppose that even now
some poignant speck of litter

borne by the river of psychic murmur
has been grafted by the brooding soul
to a beloved piece of music,

and that from the general plaint
a shape is about to be made, though
maybe not: we can't see into

the soul the way we can into
that cottage where now they're done with food
until next meal. Here's what I think:

the soul in the woods is not alone.
All he came there to leave behind
is in him, like a garrison

in a conquered city. When he goes
back to it, and goes gratefully
because it's nearly time for dinner,

he will be entering himself,
though when he faced the woods,
from the road, that's what he thought then, too.

# W.S. Merwin

■

## THE LAST ONE

Well they'd made up their minds to be everywhere because why not.
Everywhere was theirs because they thought so.
They with two leaves they whom the birds despise.
In the middle of stones they made up their minds.
They started to cut.

Well they cut everything because why not.
Everything was theirs because they thought so.
It fell into its shadows and they took both away.
Some to have some for burning.

Well cutting everything they came to the water.
They came to the end of the day there was one left standing.
They would cut it tomorrow they went away.
The night gathered in the last branches.
The shadow of the night gathered in the shadow on the water.
The night and the shadow put on the same head.
And it said Now.

Well in the morning they cut the last one.
Like the others the last one fell into its shadow.
It fell into its shadow on the water.
They took it away its shadow stayed on the water.

Well they shrugged they started trying to get the shadow away.
They cut right to the ground the shadow stayed whole.
They laid boards on it the shadow came out on top.
They shone lights on it the shadow got blacker and clearer.
They exploded the water the shadow rocked.
They built a huge fire on the roots.
They sent up black smoke between the shadow and the sun.
The new shadow flowed without changing the old one.
They shrugged they went away to get stones.

They came back the shadow was growing.
They started setting up stones it was growing.
They looked the other way it went on growing.
They decided they would make a stone out of it.
They took stones to the water they poured them into the shadow.
They poured them in they poured them in the stones vanished.
The shadow was not filled it went on growing.
That was one day.

The next day was just the same it went on growing.
They did all the same things it was just the same.
They decided to take its water from under it.
They took away water they took it away the water went down.
The shadow stayed where it was before.
It went on growing it grew onto the land.
They started to scrape the shadow with machines.
When it touched the machines it stayed on them.
They started to beat the shadow with sticks.
Where it touched the sticks it stayed on them.
They started to beat the shadow with hands.
Where it touched the hands it stayed on them.
That was another day.

Well the next day started about the same it went on growing.
They pushed lights into the shadow.
Where the shadow got onto them they went out.
They began to stomp on the edge it got their feet.
And when it got their feet they fell down.
It got into eyes the eyes went blind.
The ones that fell down it grew over and they vanished.
The ones that went blind and walked into it vanished.
The ones that could see and stood still
It swallowed their shadows.
Then it swallowed them too and they vanished.
Well the others ran.

The ones that were left went away to live if it would let them.
They went as far as they could.
The lucky ones with their shadows.


# FOR A COMING EXTINCTION

Gray whale
Now that we are sending you to The End
That great god
Tell him
That we who follow you invented forgiveness
And forgive nothing

I write as though you could understand
And I could say it
One must always pretend something
Among the dying
When you have left the seas nodding on their stalks
Empty of you
Tell him that we were made
On another day

The bewilderment will diminish like an echo
Winding along your inner mountains
Unheard by us
And find its way out
Leaving behind it the future
Dead
And ours

When you will not see again
The whale calves trying the light
Consider what you will find in the black garden
And its court
The sea cows the Great Auks the gorillas
The irreplaceable hosts ranged countless
And fore-ordaining as stars
Our sacrifices
Join your word to theirs
Tell him
That it is we who are important


## PLACE

On the last day of the world
I would want to plant a tree

what for
not for the fruit

the tree that bears the fruit
is not the one that was planted

I want the tree that stands
in the earth for the first time

with the sun already
going down

and the water
touching its roots

in the earth full of the dead
and the clouds passing

one by one
over its leaves

# Czeslaw Milosz

∎

## RIVERS

*translated by Robert Hass and Renata Gorczynski*

Under various names, I have praised only you, rivers!

You are milk and honey and love and death and dance.

From a spring in hidden grottoes, seeping from mossy rocks

Where a goddess pours live water from a pitcher,

At clear streams in the meadow, where rills murmur underground,

Your race and my race begin, and amazement, and quick passage.

Naked, I exposed my face to the sun, steering with hardly a dip of the  paddle—

Oak woods, fields, a pine forest skimming by,

Around every bend the promise of the earth,

Village smoke, sleepy herds, flights of martins over sandy bluffs.

I entered your waters slowly, step by step,

And the current in that silence took me by the knees

Until I surrendered and it carried me and I swam

Through the huge reflected sky of a triumphant noon.

I was on your banks at the onset of midsummer night

When the full moon rolls out and lips touch in the rituals of kissing—

I hear in myself, now as then, the lapping of water by the boathouse

And the whisper that calls me in for an embrace and for consolation.

We go down with the bells ringing in all the sunken cities.

Forgotten, we are greeted by the embassies of the dead,

While your endless flowing carries us on and on;

And neither is nor was. The moment only, eternal.

*Berkeley, 1980*

# Leslie Norris

## DECOYS

### 1

They work in garages,
in cold sheds behind houses,
in basements under harsh lights,
the men who make decoys.

At desks, or behind
the wheels of trucks,
all day their hands have ached
for this. They eat slowly,

savour their last cups,
and in a dream, breath
masked from the snuff of wood,
go now to set the false birds

free. Their saws are warm
and humming, their burrs,
their files, rotate
at an electric wish.

Everywhere is a fur
of dust; of walnut,
of white oak, logged forests
dried for this making.

With the flat of their palms
they measure the neck's right curve
and set with an eye
an angle to the beak.

Such birds must look comfortable.
The glass eyes are inserted
in a parody of safety,
neither wild nor mad.

Now it is the caress
of repetitive fine abrasives
transforms to feathers
the annual rings, to a persuasion of down.

The paint is brilliant,
acrylic, quick-drying,
more accurate than nature.
It is touched with shadows.

There are seven shades of black.

2

Such perfect creatures keep
at the edges of your mind.
They will not breed, are mere
flawless images. Let them bob
in the ebb of your knowledge.

Soon you will forget them.
White-fronts out of Spitzbergen,
flying through sleet cold enough
to freeze the soft tongues in their mouths,
would find your decoys faulty:

yet you can tease them down
with a sheet of newsprint,
torn like a heart and weighed
with a clod of grass. Set it
blunt end to the wind, and watch

the great birds from the sea
come flighting in. But the best,
the most killing, of all deceits,
is a dead bird. Keep the few
unbroken of your last deaths. Place them

pale breasts to the sky, heads
to the wind; and let them lie
on the cold saltings,
on scatterings of snow no whiter
than the fans of their tails.

Do this alone, on a night
no other man would walk in,
wary of ice in your gun-barrels,
the tide shifting, the light
blown all ways of the compass.

You must be still as a dead bird.

3

The gun has its knowledge, its action
fast as instinct. Once, on an empty night,
our sacks still folded, a heavy dew
an hour away with the dawn,
my gun swung in its own smooth curve,
pulling my hands to fire.
There was not a pause.

And the mallard fell out of darkness
in its weight, its feathered heaviness.

It was a green drake. I took it from the ditch
as its eye faded. By god, said my friend, dancing,
you scraped it off the face of the moon.
I brushed the wing that had pushed night from under it.

It was the gun had known.

4

There are men, they are born with it,
who have the gift of calling.

They live in cottages on the saltings,
or if in villages, move quietly by night.

Nothing changes in their country but they know it;
the angle of a gate, a dropped branch, shifts in the wind.

For them the sky fills with wildfowl. The lanes of flight
clamour for them, for them sanderling

and redshank patter at the tide's withdrawing runnels.
They turn, in quiet beds, at a flake of snow.

When they call, when they squat in a hide
or hide in a thick of bush,

they blow through cupped hands
for a meeting of animals and birds.

Call again and again, the note rising,
an elegy for vulnerable creatures,

the hare, the partridge, runners and low fliers.
And for the waterbirds, for rafts of teal,

the pied shelduck, for skeins of geese,
brent goose, snow goose, pinkfoot, Canada,

the little bean goose, hardy in the air,
the royal swan, the whooper,

all humble on land, on their pliable webs.
Let the men put away rapacious lead, let them be still.

The birds have given them the wide, cold sky,
they have given them dreams of innocence,

they have given them voices.

# Sharon Olds

∎

## THE UNDERLIFE

Waiting for the subway, bad station, no one near me, the
walls dark and slimy, waiting in the
bowel heart of the city, I look down
into the pit where the train rides
and see a section of grey rail de-
tach itself and move along the packed silt
floor of the pit. It is the first rat I have
seen on the subway in twenty years and at
first a shudder runs over me as
naturally as wind ripples water in the
upper world of light, I draw back, but then I
think of my son's mice and lean forward—this is
wild-life, the ones who survive in the city
as if it were a ruin. And the rat is smallish, not
big as a cat like those rats that eat babies, it is
ash-grey and although it must be
filthy it doesn't look greasy but rather
silvery and filth-fluffy, and though its
ears are black you can see the slightest bit of
dark light through them as if under the steel-dust they're
translucent. It glides along the side of the rail, it does
not look bitter or malicious, it does not look evil, just
cautious and domestic, innocent
as a lion is innocent. Back home I
wash and wash my hands and get into
bed with a book, and as I sink down
calmly to read, a part of the amber
pattern on the sheet detaches itself and
moves as if a tiny bit of the
earth's crust were moving—Christ I
slap at it crying out You jerk! You jerk!
and of course it's a cockroach, minion of the night city,
has lived in the ruins of all the cities
before their razing and after it.
Christ you guys, I address these beasts, I
know about the dark floor of life shifting!
I watched the cancer take my father and
alter him so he did not fit the
space he was set in, I saw that cancer
wiggle him like a bad tooth and
finally tear him out of the picture so I
saw the blank behind him, I know all this! And the
roach and the rat turn to me with that
swivelling turn of natural animals and they
say to me, We are not educators,
we come to you from him, to bring you his love.

# Robert Pack

∎

## WATCHERS

*Photographed from the moon, [the Earth] seems to be*
*a kind of organism. It is plainly in the process of*
*developing, like an enormous embryo. It is, for all its*
*stupendous size and the numberless units of its life forms,*
*coherent. Every tissue is linked for its viability to every*
*other tissue.*

—Lewis Thomas, *The Medusa and the Snail*

And so I'm linked to you
like cells within a growing embryo,
        and you are linked to me,
and we, together, linked to everyone
        as watchers from the moon can see.

The patient watchers from the moon can tell
        what currents pushing through the tide
direct vast spawnings from the swaying deep,
        and what ancestral pathways
through the buoyant air wedged wild geese keep

        inscribed within their brains
that safely store stupendous images—
        range after range of mountain snow,
        and shadowed woodland green,
blue sky reflected in blue sea below.

        Although they see all parts as one,
wholly dependent and yet numberless,
        the watchers from the moon
surmise some flaw may be developing,
        some rampant cells may soon

outgrow the rest, as if they knew their lives
        were all life meant. And yet, at least
for now, the watchers from the moon are full
        of admiration, awe,
each tissue seems connected, viable—

like you and me, together,
linked as one with our increasing kind,
    taking dominion everywhere,
now cultivating forests, now the seas,
    now blasting even through the air.

    The membrane of the sky
holds in accumulated oxygen,
    welcomes the visible, good light,
protects from lethal ultraviolet,
        and guards against the flight

of random meteors that burn out,
harmless at the edge of our home space, as if
        by miracle, although
just friction from our atmosphere is what
    the watchers from the moon must know

    keeps us alive and linked
each to the other, each to the sunlit cycles
    of exhaling plants and trees.
For pollination, fruits and flowers have
    warm winds and their obliging bees;

forests renew themselves from their decay,
    aided by intermittent rain;
and plankton, drifting in the sun to breed,
    provide the herring and the whale
        with all the food they need

    to keep revolving life alive
        in this appointed place—
to which we're linked and which replenishes
        ambrosia of the air
    and animates the sea that says

    *Coherence is the law*
*We must obey*, although the watchers see
    certain relentless cells below,
dividing, and divided from the rest,
    forming a monster embryo.

# Alan Michael Parker

∎

## MUD

A blur of elements, a cataract
of sod—the canyon sloughs its juniper
and sagebrush with a shrug. High tension wires
snap: blue sparks sizzle to the ridge and back.

Beyond the barn, the Dodge, the ambulance
and firetruck; past the flush of volunteers,
cheese sandwiches and coffee, sacraments
of natural disaster, slumps the Owner.

He'll rise. He'll take his slicker from the fence
and join the wake, his house and pond and shed
—goddamnit his tomatoes—choked with mud.
And still he thinks: *There are no accidents.*

His property, his body. All that is
or will be mud, and loss, and artifice.

# Michael Pettit

∎

## NEAT NEW ENGLAND FIELDS

With his lopping shears, double-bladed axe,
and bow saw, John Wylie's out to take back
his field from the scrub cedar and sumac

grown up these years he's labored for wages
and not on the land his father had clear,
had *green with corn high as a man could reach.*

Each tangle of briars damns John Wylie,
his sad neglect, his letting go acres
of earth to the earth's own poor purposes.

He's out there in the cold, pipe in his teeth,
axe in his hands, attacking all the years
he's lost and wants back now his life is his.

He must feel every blow recovers
a day, a week, and when the white birch falls
he again has that far hillside corner

he had as a child. It is where he hid
from his father's hard voice, from all the chores
a child hates and a man makes his life of.

It is salvation, this neat destruction
John Wylie and the good New England folk
wreak upon the land. And how I hate it,

hate the green fields all in perfect order,
hate the old stone fences that won't fall down,
hate the houses and barns in good repair,

hate the yews and privet trimmed just so,
hate the tidy flowerbeds I too tend,
hate the leaves I rake from their resting place.

What I want back is not the simple past,
not my lost life, but my life going on,
growing like some wild weed in the neat field.

Like dandelion, milkweed, chicory,
I want to strike root without design,
wherever the wind blows the tiny seed.

I want to send out runners through the earth
and rank growth above, green shoots too vital
for the man with the axe to clear away.

I want him to leave shaking his head, lost
as when he began, as we are all lost
unless we let our lives go, and follow.

# Stanley Plumly

∎

## LAPSED MEADOW

*for James Wright*


Wild has its skills.
   The apple grew so close to the ground
it seemed the whole tree
     was thicket, crab and root—

    by fall it looked
like brush among burdock and hawkweed;
looked as if brush had been piled,
    for burning, at the center.

    At the edges, blurred,
like failed fence, the hawthorns, by
comparison, seemed planted.
    Everywhere else there was broom

     grass and timothy
and wood fern and sometimes a sapling,
sometimes a run of hazel. In Ohio,
    some people call it

    a farmer's field, all fireweed
and thistle, a waste of nature. And true,
you could lose yourself
    in the mind of the thing,

    especially summer, in the full
sun or later, after rain and the smell
of rain—you could lose
    yourself, waist- or head-high,

    branch by leaf by branch.
There could be color, the kind that opens
and the kind that closes up,
    one for each part

    of the light; there might
be fruit, green or grounded—it was always
skin-tight, small and hard.
    There would be goldenrod

            still young or yellowing
        in season, and wind enough to seed a countryside
of plows and pasture.
            But I call it crazy

            the way that apple,
        in the middle of a field, dug in, part of the year
bare-knuckled, part of the year
            blossoming.


## Chinese Tallow

I wanted to put the tree in the room,
the way the light in the morning
first fills, then surrounds it,
the way the light this morning brings it
to the window, brings it in, almost into the room.
And I wanted to bring the rain in with it,
the rain from all day yesterday, all night
until just now, the light filling the rain,
filled with the rain, the rain the light on the tree.

I did not want to wake in a room empty with air.
I did not want the shadow of the tree, blind sun.
I did not want the smell of it sweet in the room.
I did not want it brought in blessed with the thought of it.
I did not want it turned into something else,
branch and spider root, wet with possibilities.
I wanted to bring it in first light, shining, here.
I wanted it large with the rain inside it, filled with rain.
I wanted to wake in a room bright with small dark leaves.

# Pattiann Rogers

∎

## SECOND WITNESS

The only function of the red-cupped fruit
Hanging from the red stem of the sassafras
Is to reveal the same shiny blue orb of berry
Existing in me.

The only purpose of the row of hemlocks blowing
On the rocky ridge is to give form to the crossed lines
And clicking twigs, the needle-leaf matrix
Of evergreen motion I have always possessed.

Vega and the ring nebula and the dust
Of the Pleiades have made clear by themselves
The constellations inherent to my eyes.

What is it I don't know of myself
From never having seen a crimson chat at its feeding
Or the dunnart carrying its young? It must be imperative
That I watch the entire hardening of the bud
Of the clove, that I witness the flying fish breaking
Into sky through the sun-smooth surface of the sea.

I ask the winter wren nesting in the clogged roots
Of the fallen oak to remember the multitoned song
Of itself in my ears, and I ask the short-snouted
Silver twig weevil to be particular and the fishhook
Cactus to be tenacious. I thank the distinct edges
Of the six-spined spider crab for their peculiarities
And praise the freshwater eel for its graces. I urge
The final entanglement of blade and light to keep
Its secrecy, and I beg the white-tailed kite this afternoon,
For my sake, to be keen-eyed, to soar well, to be quick
To make me known.

# THE HUMMINGBIRD: A SEDUCTION

If I were a female hummingbird perched still
And quiet on an upper myrtle branch
In the spring afternoon and if you were a male
Alone in the whole heavens before me, having parted
Yourself, for me, from cedar top and honeysuckle stem
And earth down, your body hovering in midair
Far away from jewelweed, thistle and bee balm;

And if I watched how you fell, plummeting before me,
And how you rose again and fell, with such mastery
That I believed for a moment *you* were the sky
And the red-marked bird diving inside your circumference
Was just the physical revelation of the light's
Most perfect desire;

And if I saw your sweeping and sucking
Performance of swirling egg and semen in the air,
The weaving, twisting vision of red petal
And nectar and soaring rump, the rush of your wing
In its grand confusion of arcing and splitting
Created completely out of nothing just for me,

Then when you came down to me, I would call you
My own spinning bloom of ruby sage, my funneling
Storm of sunlit sperm and pollen, my only breathless
Piece of scarlet sky, and I would bless the base
Of each of your feathers and touch the tine
Of string muscles binding your wings and taste
The odor of your glistening oils and hunt
The honey in your crimson flare
And I would take you and take you and take you
Deep into any kind of nest you ever wanted.

# Eulogy for a Hermit Crab

You were consistently brave
On these surf-drenched rocks, in and out of their salty
Slough holes around which the entire expanse
Of the glinting grey sea and the single spotlight
Of the sun went spinning and spinning and spinning
In a tangle of blinding spume and spray
And pistol-shot collisions your whole life long.
You stayed. Even with the wet icy wind of the moon
Circling your silver case night after night after night
You were here.

And by the gritty orange curve of your claws,
By the soft, wormlike grip
Of your hinter body, by the unrelieved wonder
Of your black-pea eyes, by the mystified swing
And swing and swing of your touching antennae,
You maintained your name meticulously, you kept
Your name intact exactly, day after day after day.
No one could say you were less than perfect
In the hermitage of your crabness.

Now, beside the racing, incomprehensible racket
Of the sea stretching its great girth forever
Back and forth between this direction and another,
Please let the words of this proper praise I speak
Become the identical and proper sound
Of my mourning.

# David St. John

∎

## IRIS

*Vivian St. John (1891—1974)*

There is a train inside this iris:

You think I'm crazy, & like to say boyish
& outrageous things. No, there is

A train inside this iris.

It's a child's finger bearded in black banners.
A single window like a child's nail,

A darkened porthole lit by the white, angular face

Of an old woman, or perhaps the boy beside her in the stuffy,
Hot compartment. Her hair is silver, & sweeps

Back off her forehead, onto her cold & bruised shoulders.

The prairies fail along Chicago. Past the five
Lakes. Into the black woods of her New York; & as I bend

Close above the iris, I see the train

Drive deep into the damp heart of its stem, & the gravel
Of the garden path

Cracks under my feet as I walk this long corridor

Of elms, arched
Like the ceiling of a French railway pier where a boy

With pale curls holding

A fresh iris is waving goodbye to a grandmother, gazing
A long time

Into the flower, as if he were looking some great

Distance, or down an empty garden path & he believes a man
Is walking toward him, working

Dull shears in one hand; & now believe me: The train
Is gone. The old woman is dead, & the boy. The iris curls,
On its stalk, in the shade

Of those elms: Where something like the icy & bitter fragrance

In the wake of a woman who's just swept past you on her way
Home

& you remain.

# Reg Saner

∎

## WAITING OUT RAIN, SHELTERED BY OVERHANG

### I

Fascinated by rains of empty joy
that slowly instructed broken river-thrones
to invest sun and moon
in the throat of a sparrowhawk,
I enter somnolent cumulus
rifted with cobalt, and fall half a mile

without harm. Then Hiamovi, Red Peak, Thatchtop
re-emerge from my breath: each summit, a vapor.

### II

Glum as self-knowledge a lone magpie puffs up
under spruce bough, shudders, then sorts itself
back into wet feathers. Mists collapse all around me
like vast bergs crashing and grinding
slower than running in dreams,
a thousand feet down. As if dismayed
an elk out of sight gives off a hurt bellow
old as the animals first discovering mankind
no longer one of them.

### III

Is any design softer spoken than fog
deciding what next to do with us?

At the back of its mind, evergreen ancients
leave and arrive. Mt. Watanga looms, distorts,
and dies where cloud drifts with a motion
quiet as the moon
crossing an unlidded eye, or mountains
too brief to believe in.

Now, amid rain's vacant sizzle on granite
and pools on a slab winking back at me,
if I steal the world's power
not to be my own body
no hush fills with more wilderness
than an eardrum, listening for itself

inside a life that once was, and still is.

# *Richard Shelton*

∎

## SONORA FOR SALE

this is the land of gods in exile
they are fragile and without pride
they require no worshipers

we come down a white road in the moonlight
dragging our feet like innocents
to find the guilty already arrived
and in possession of everything

we see the stars as they were years ago
but for us it is the future
they warn us too late

we are here we cannot turn back
soon we hold out our hands
full of money
this is the desert
it is all we have left to destroy

# GLEN CANYON ON THE COLORADO

*Past these towering monuments, past these mounded*
*billows of orange sandstone, past these oak-set*
*glens, past these fern-decked alcoves, past these*
*mural caves, we glide hour after hour, stopping*
*now and then, as our attention is arrested by*
*some new wonder, until we reach a point which is*
*historic.*

—John Wesley Powell

1

soon it will be thirty-five years
since the gamblers passed a leather cup
from hand to hand
some breathing into it for luck
some passing it on quickly
as though it burned

and we said we have been told
it is necessary we said we have waited
long enough let us have
the comfort we deserve and whatever
profit can be earned from it
though it brings darkness
to remote places no one is there

let there be announcements
by those who announce let it be done
let it be over let the rain come
and the water rise
let there be no more talk
of monuments in a distant wilderness
we will create new monuments
to our own ability
we will move over the water
with such speed we will forget
even what we have never known

surely our time has come
let them gather the waters together
and create a lake in the desert
for our pleasure

then we heard the distant
explosions of dice and it was over
that which was reprieved was reprieved
for a while and that which was damned
was damned forever

2

once there was a canyon
where the river was lying down
resting for a while from all its labors
moving in repose past hanging gardens
of ferns and monkey flowers
and sheltered groves of box elders

where in the golden light
of cottonwood and autumn sun
the canyon wren would flirt
with anyone who came along
staying just ahead moving in and out
among polished driftwood and stones
promising something wonderful
around the next bend *follow follow*
she called with a voice as low
and liquid as any siren's song

where sometimes the shadow of a heron
would hoist itself above the water
flapping its wings
as though they needed oiling
while the determined beaver
followed his nose in a straight line
going somewhere important upstream
his silver wake spreading behind him

and at night when the cliffs
seemed to lean inward over the river
like giant black guardians
protecting stone cathedrals from the moon
and the beaver slept in lodges
so close to the surface they could hear
every word the river said
and all that the willows replied
a brilliant ribbon of stars
would unwind itself above the cliffs
following each turn of the canyon walls

soon that place will no longer exist
in the memory of anyone living
and will be hinted at only in photographs
and in the dim visions of words
as untrustworthy as our own

when we say *at this point in time*
to avoid the terror of saying *now*
the unredeemable moment where we live
with all past actions beyond our reach
and sinking down through dark water

3

once there was a canyon
just another canyon on the Colorado
saddest of all the poor
damned rivers of the West

soon it will be thirty-five years
since we passed that point in time
which was historic
since we crossed a dark meridian
from which there is no return

and we drift we drift
on a lake of our own making
casting our offerings upon the water
our cans and bottles
the detritus of careless lives
and we watch our calendars
float away and sink slowly downward
one month at a time into a world
drowned for our good reasons

where a few fish swim
through the ghostly branches
of dead cottonwoods where there is no
season no sunlight on sandstone
no song of the canyon wren nor any sound

where the bones of those
who were not historic
sit under the floors of their houses
in baskets while the stones
of their walls fall silently in
and black silt covers everything

4

where have you gone
bright spirit of that canyon
numen of secret gardens and hidden groves
who balanced the sunlight
on one palisaded wall
against the shadow on the other

whose voice was the little wind
playing among the oak leaves
or the strong wind of a storm
winding down the canyon as a warning
or the invitation of the canyon wren
or the dove's cooing

and will we see you again
as we drift on in darkness
followed by the moon's white face
floating on the surface of our lake
like the ghost of some dead thing

will we who never saw you
see your likes again
when we sink into the silk of earth
or when our ashes rock for a moment
on the surface of the water
perhaps the surface of a lake
of our own making before sliding down
will we know then at last
that we have always been blind
and will we see then what is gone
beyond all seeing

5

sink softly down
black silt to the canyon floor
as flower petals fall
as motes of sunlight drift through air
and settle in the evening
when the wind is still
sink softly down
fill the canyon from wall to wall

fall gently rain
upon the surface of this lake
shine softly moon and stars
it is no mirror for your light
it is the tomb of beauty
lost forever
and it is despair
the darkness in ourselves we fear

# Charles Simic

∎

## STRICTLY BUCOLIC

*for Mark and Jules*

Are these mellifluous sheep,
And these the meadows made twice-melliferous by their
    bleating?
Is that the famous mechanical wind-up shepherd
Who comes with instructions and service manual?

This must be the regulation white fleece
Bleached and starched to perfection,
And we could be posing for our first communion pictures,
Except for the nasty horns.

I am beginning to think this might be
The Angelic Breeders Association's
Millennial Company Picnic (all expenses paid)
With a few large black dogs as special guests.

These dogs serve as ushers and usherettes.
They're always studying the rules,
The exigencies of proper deportment
When they're not reading Theocritus,

Or wagging their tails at the approach of
Theodora. Or is it Theodosius? Or even Theodoric?
They're theomorfic, of course. They theologize.
Theogony is their favorite. They also love theomachy.

Now they hand out the blue ribbons.
Ah, there's one for everyone!
Plus the cauldrons of stinking cabbage and boiled turnips
Which don't figure in this idyll.

# A Landscape with Crutches

So many crutches. Now even the daylight
Needs one, even the smoke
As it goes up. And the shacks—
One per customer—they move off
In a single file with difficulty,

I said, with a hell of an effort . . .
And the trees behind them about to stumble,
And the ants on their toy-crutches,
And the wind on its ghost-crutch.

I can't get any peace around here:
The bread on its artificial limbs,
A headless doll in a wheelchair,
And my mother, mind you, using
Two knives for crutches as she squats to pee.

# Maurya Simon

∎

## THE SADNESS OF RIVERS

The sadness of rivers is their aimlessness.
Though the edge of the world invites them,
they refuse to go beyond themselves.
Even the wolves of destiny can't persuade them
to forsake the lyric poem for the epic.

The contentment of trees is their protocol;
always bowing good-day, waving good-bye,
they make a ceremony out of greening.
They even put up with the coal-hearted crow,
with ruptured kites, and an armor of snow.

The bitterness of mountains is a solid fire,
banked and fueled by an envy of clouds.
With hearts of granite, mountains are unmoved
by the sight of swans reshaping the skies,
by the slow deaths of free-wheeling stars.

The joy of roses is a breaking of silence;
their fragrance a translation of light.
Their marvelous bodies spell out desire
in the coldest years of exile, when hunger
sings in the ice and despair licks itself.

The wisdom of oceans is a holy invention.
Though waves love to confess their passions
to unlistening shores, the ancient scrolls
of spindrift retain their pearly secrets,
the waters of oblivion seal their doors.

The gratitude of stones is wide as the world.
Their shadows are heirlooms the day hoards,
along with the blessings of pebbles.
Stones know the words under our tongues
are their children: mutable, jagged, bold.

# Atomic Psalm

Last night the stars seemed not themselves,
for they sang such a lonely song
I heard all creation weep along.
And the moon seemed too molten hot—
it burned a hole right through the roof,
right through the sky, it burned
an empty place into the night.

And oh how the world rocked
like a cradle in the ether of the dark.
And how the children, lost in dreams,
awoke with a start, not out of fear
but from surprise. They blinked their eyes
in that starless night, that moonless night,
and cried, though no one heard.

God-Who-Is-Not, give us a lock
of your immortal hair, or give us stars
that we can reach and hang upon the bars
of our despair; give us back the rock
called moon, that still, white face
we write our lives upon. Give us back
our dark hope in its golden case.


# FROM SPELLBOUND: AN ALPHABET

It is February in the mountains
    and the snow falls lazily
        for hours upon chinks
            of chain-linked
                fence, so
                    each

builds its own small, pubic V
    of white powder, a signal
        to us who want them:
            winter touches
                everything,
                    thus

silence accrues crystal by
    crystal in the cities,
        too, and it lodges
            subtly out of
                view in
                    sand,

where stands of cactus hold
hands stiffly, barbed
statues who await
deliverance, a
sudden glow
of ice.

Here snow falls openly as if
what's secret in a world
is prisoned in what
we see descend,
as if each
web

shelters a seed of history, an
intricate tale respun again
and trapped in a like
transience as ours
which gravity
coaxes

down and that melts away before
we can reclaim it, before
we've gathered in air
or exhaled loss,
or tasted a
drop.

Branches balance the snowy cape
along pinegreen, open arms
as bark bustles in warmth
and a bird goes about
its own business,
breaking

up the silence with forsaken cries,
while the clouds' black orchards
overhead unheave, unloosen the
ice-lacquered petals, frozen
syllables, the tiny veils
of knowing and unknown,
of the endless cold,
of all sorrows, of
everything old &
forgotten and
everything
reborn.

# Dave Smith

∎

## LEAFLESS TREES, CHICKAHOMINY SWAMP

Humorless, hundreds of trunks, gray in the blue expanse
where dusk leaves them hacked like a breastwork,
stripped like pikes planted to impale, the knots
of vines at each groin appearing placed by makers
schooled in grotesque campaigns. Mathew Brady's
plates show them as they are, the ageless stumps,
time-sanded solitaries, some clumped in squads
we might imagine veterans, except they're only wood,
and nothing in the world seems more dead than these.

Stopped by the lanes filled with homebound taillights,
we haven't seen the rumored Eagle we hoped to watch,
only a clutch of buzzards ferrying sticks for a nest.
Is this history, that we want the unchanged, useless
spines out there to thrust in our faces the human
qualities we covet? We read this place like generals
whose promised recruits don't show, unable to press on:
there is the languor of battle, troops who can't tell
themselves from the enemy, and file-hard fear gone

indifferent in the mortaring sun that will leave them
night after night standing in the same cold planes
of water. It never blooms or greens. It merely stinks.
Why can't we admit it's death, blameless, say that
festering scummy scene is nothing but a blown brainpan?
Why do we sit and sniff the rank hours keeping words
full of ground that only stares off our question: what
happened? Leaf-light in our heads, don't we mean why
these grisly emblems, the slime that won't swell to hope?

The rapacious odor of swamps all over the earth bubbles
sometimes to mist, fetid flesh we can't see but know
as cells composing, decomposing, illusions of the heart.
God knows what we'd do in there, we say, easing back
on the blacktop. Once we heard a whistling. Harmonicas?
But who'd listen? Surely all was green once, fragile
as a truce, words braiding sun and water, as on a lake
where families sang. What else would we hope for, do
in the dead miles nothing explains or changes or relieves?

# Gary Snyder

∎

## PIUTE CREEK

One granite ridge
A tree, would be enough
Or even a rock, a small creek,
A bark shred in a pool.
Hill beyond hill, folded and twisted
Tough trees crammed
In thin stone fractures
A huge moon on it all, is too much.
The mind wanders. A million
Summers, night air still and the rocks
Warm.   Sky over endless mountains.
All the junk that goes with being human
Drops away, hard rock wavers
Even the heavy present seems to fail
This bubble of a heart.
Words and books
Like a small creek off a high ledge
Gone in the dry air.

A clear, attentive mind
Has no meaning but that
Which sees is truly seen.
No one loves rock, yet we are here.
Night chills. A flick
In the moonlight
Slips into Juniper shadow:
Back there unseen
Cold proud eyes
Of Cougar or Coyote
Watch me rise and go.

# THE REAL WORK
*(Today with Zach & Dan rowing by Alcatraz and around Angel Island)*

sea-lions and birds,
sun through fog
flaps up and lolling,
looks you dead in the eye.
sun haze;
a long tanker riding light and high.

sharp wave choppy line—
interface tide-flows—
seagulls sit on the meeting
eating;
we slide by white-stained cliffs.

the real work.
washing and sighing,
sliding by.


# FOR ALL

Ah to be alive
       on a mid-September morn
       fording a stream
       barefoot, pants rolled up,
       holding boots, pack on,
       sunshine, ice in the shallows,
       northern Rockies.

Rustle and shimmer of icy creek waters
stones turn underfoot, small and hard as toes
       cold nose dripping
       singing inside
       creek music, heart music,
       smell of sun on gravel.

       I pledge allegiance.

I pledge allegiance to the soil
       of Turtle Island,
       one ecosystem
       in diversity
       under the sun
With joyful interpenetration for all.

# Marcia Southwick

∎

## THE MARSH

Each time I return to this place
I expect to find a recurring distance
between myself and the huge trees,
as though I were in a dream
in which I could run toward them forever
and never get there.

Right now the marsh seems unfamiliar
because the crickets have taken me by surpirse;
their singing has entered my mind just now,
even though I've been hearing them all along.
So I'm almost afraid,
because there must be other ways
in which I am left out of the landscape—
It's as if the mallards stay hidden in the grass
for a purpose. But I don't think they are there
to make me understand what I don't already know,
only to point out how often I'm surprised.
And that is why the mallards fly suddenly upward,
leaving the grass empty and essential.

And when I try to summarize the difference
between the tide and the way I remember it,
I find myself unable to explain
all that I have discarded—
The driftwood, fish skeletons
and chipped shells
are remnants of a past life
I can't possibly understand.

# William Stafford

∎

## CEREMONY

On the third finger of my left hand
under the bank of the Ninnescah
a muskrat whirled and bit to the bone.
The mangled hand made the water red.

That was something the ocean would remember:
I saw me in the current flowing through the land,
rolling, touching roots, the world incarnadined,
and the river richer by a kind of marriage.

While in the woods an owl started quavering
with drops like tears I raised my arm.
Under the bank a muskrat was trembling
with meaning my hand would wear forever.

In that river my blood flowed on.


## IN RESPONSE TO A QUESTION

The earth says have a place, be what that place
requires; hear the sound the birds imply
and see as deep as ridges go behind
each other. (Some people call their scenery flat,
their only picture framed by what they know:
I think around them rise a riches and a loss
too equal for their chart—but absolutely tall.)

The earth says every summer have a ranch
that's minimum: one tree, one well, a landscape
that proclaims a universe—sermon
of the hills, hallelujah mountain,
highway guided by the way the world is tilted,
reduplication of mirage, flat evening:
a kind of ritual for the wavering.

The earth says where you live wear the kind
of color that your life is (gray shirt for me)
and by listening with the same bowed head that sings
draw all into one song, join

the sparrow on the lawn, and row that easy
way, the rage without met by the wings
within that guide you anywhere the wind blows.

Listening, I think that's what the earth says.

## B. C.

The seed that met water spoke a little name.

(Great sunflowers were lording the air that day;
this was before Jesus, before Rome; that other air
was readying our hundreds of years to say things
that rain has beat down on over broken stones
and heaped behind us in many slag lands.)

Quiet in the earth a drop of water came,
and the little seed spoke: "Sequoia is my name."

## FALL WIND

Pods of summer crowd around the door;
I take them in the autumn of my hands.

Last night I heard the first cold wind outside;
the wind blew soft, and yet I shiver twice:

Once for thin walls, once for the sound of time.

# *Ruth Stone*

∎

## SNOW TRIVIA

In secret molecules
snow is going back into the sky.
From edge to edge
the glacier pauses; midwinter thaw.

Snow is more air than water.
Buried alive under its crystals
you might live for days.

One year in Vermont
sheep herders froze in July
during a freak snowstorm.

Road commissioners, intercoms,
snowplows at three a.m.
booming like Civil War cannons.
On the ski trails
wax and more wax. Pole uphill.
Ski racks on compacts,
front wheel drive.

When the airport in Tehran
imploded under four feet of snow,
a survivor said she felt only
a cold tremor before the roof came down.

The study of snowflakes can
be an interdepartmental discipline.

Before pollution, mothers created
ice cream by adding sugar and vanilla
to fresh snow.

                Snow is deceptive.
Even in Nepal where the Abominable is,
the doomed climbers trapped
on a narrow ledge
which helicopters could not reach,
continued to be seen waving
and lighting flares
against the mountain until
they were blotted out
by snowfall.

# LAGUNA BEACH

The shingle roofs burgeon moss, green as tender acacia.
Under their eaves giant roses in cinemascope flash
Over-developed boobs; huge green penises rise, hairy,
Bristling with impotence, into trees that hold them.
Meanwhile the trees wait around on one foot for a place
To set the penises aside. It rains.
The sun draws off all the water.
Nature says yes to everything.

# *Arthur Sze*

∎

## PARALLAX

*"Kwakwha."*
*"Askwali."*
The shift in Hopi when a man or woman says "thank you"
becomes a form of parallax.
A man travels

from Mindanao to Kyushu and says his inner geography
is enlarged by each new place.
Is it?
Might he not grow more by staring for twenty four hours
at a single pine needle?

I watch a woman tip an ashtray and empty
a few ashes into her mouth,
but ah, I want
other soliloquies.
I want equivalents to Chu-ko Liang sending his fire ships

downstream into Ts'ao Ts'ao's fleet.
It does not mean
a geneticist must quit
and devote his life to the preservation of rhinoceros,
but it might mean

watching a thousand snow geese drift on water
as the sky darkens minute by minute.
*"Kwakwha,"*
*"askwali,"*
whenever, wherever.

# Nathaniel Tarn

∎

## FROM JOURNAL OF THE LAGUNA DE SAN IGNACIO

Immense architecture
building in air
towers and palaces
from which their eyes look out,
star denizens
living in the heights
as they live below
building in air
and undersea
their passage through our life—
         a gentle glide
like a dream
because no thing men know
so huge and gentle at once
can be other than dream
    in such a world.
Whales breathing
all around us in the night
just beyond the lights,
ghost gulls
following the ship
which seems to breathe
yet never moves
against the great Pacific's
unfathomable shoulders

∎

The mountains rise out of the desert
way out over Baja
the whales rise out of the sea
the mountains rise out of the sea
the whales rise out of the desert
the whales are taller than the mountains

∎

Dazzle of light
pale mountains, pale dunes
pale clouds on pale blue skies
immense skullcap of light over the whole,
         the sea fetching sighs
  under the skiff,
his heart

folded among the sea's pages—
        from the depths coming up
   in musical surf
arched bow of the whale
    the vertebrae
shining through skin
circling the skiff
passing, they say,
the flukes over his head
so fast he did not see them
(though they were larger than his houseroof)
but felt the hair on his head
lie down which the wind had raised.
        And the heart came up also
which, in its fear,
the sea had previously bound into its secrets


∎


Forest of whales,
Lebanon cedars
with their roots in the sea
sparring,
looking down at leisure
on the human world.
Forest of heads
above the prophet
in his rubber coffin,
laid out with all his jewels
tight round his neck,
his escaping soul's
breath still alive
is the finest mist
among the clouds of spray
from the cruising whales,
you will recognize it

# Alberta Turner

∎

## Small Animal

have I found you?
Your den is narrow, has many holes,
but earth is hollow under the spruce log
and bare by the white stone,
and grass is broken on the bank.

Snow has lain two days now, and no tracks.
You're warm or asleep or afraid.

Yet I'm no trap.
If I knew your food, I'd bring it.
I'd kill for you
whom I've never seen.

I'd put my arm deep into your den,
who are my only chance
for a wet nose in the hand
or teeth.

# Lee Upton

∎

## Water Gardening

What could anyone want from the water poppies,
the integuments or the heart-shaped
leaves of the milky-sapped aquatics,
iris and marsh marigold?
What have I wanted from the brown
china marks moth and the ribbon grass,
swamp lobelia and wapato and bee balm? I couldn't
have seen anyone floating
in the tea-colored shadows, spreading
as water mosses, as the brain's pickerel weed.
If I lower myself I can see
the nerves of water, the freshwater whelk's red
jelly eggs, the roots of a flossy lily,
the wind blowing these fine skins back,
stirring the garden into canals, more nerves, rootlets—
until some gnat-like little botherer rises to pester
my arm and head. He is trying so hard
to deliver his delirium
deliriously, his one eyelash—as if to say,
I can't leave you and I can't stay—of wisdom.

# Ellen Bryant Voigt

∎

## THE BAT

Reading in bed, full of sentiment
for the mild evening and the children
asleep in adjacent rooms, hearing them
cry out now and then the brief reports
of sufficient imagination, and listening
at the same time compassionately
to the scrabble of claws, the fast treble
in the chimney—
                  then it was out,
not a trapped bird
beating at the seams of the ceiling,
but a bat lifting toward us, falling away.

*Dominion over every living thing,*
*large brain, a choice of weapons—*
Shuddering, in the lit hall
we swung repeatedly against
its rising secular face
until it fell; then
shoveled it into the yard for the cat
who shuttles easily between two worlds.

# David Wagoner

∎

## LOST

Stand still. The trees ahead and bushes beside you
Are not lost. Wherever you are is called Here,
And you must treat it as a powerful stranger,
Must ask permission to know it and be known.
The forest breathes. Listen. It answers,
I have made this place around you.
If you leave it, you may come back again, saying Here.
No two trees are the same to Raven.
No two branches are the same to Wren.
If what a tree or a bush does is lost on you,
You are surely lost. Stand still. The forest knows
Where you are. You must let it find you.

## MEETING A BEAR

If you haven't made noise enough to warn him, singing, shouting,
Or thumping sticks against trees as you walk in the woods,
Giving him time to vanish
(As he wants to) quietly sideways through the nearest thicket,
You may wind up standing face to face with a bear.
Your near future,
Even your distant future, may depend on how he feels
Looking at you, on what he makes of you
And your upright posture
Which, in his world, like a down-swayed head and humped shoulders,
Is a standing offer to fight for territory
And a mate to go with it.
Gaping and staring directly are as risky as running:
To try for dominance or moral authority
Is an empty gesture,
And taking to your heels is an invitation to a dance
Which, from your point of view, will be no circus.
He won't enjoy your smell
Or anything else about you, including your ancestors
Or the shape of your snout. If the feeling's mutual,
It's still out of balance:
He doesn't *care* what you think or calculate; your disapproval
Leaves him as cold as the opinions of salmon.
He may feel free
To act out all his own displeasures with a vengeance:
You would do well to try your meekest behavior,

155

Standing still
As long as you're not mauled or hugged, your eyes downcast.
But if you must make a stir, do everything sidelong,
Gently and naturally,
Vaguely oblique. Withdraw without turning and start saying
Softly, monotonously, whatever comes to mind
Without special pleading:
Nothing hurt or reproachful to appeal to his better feelings.
He has none, only a harder life than yours.
There's no use singing
National anthems or battle hymns or alma maters
Or any other charming or beastly music.
Use only the dullest,
Blandest, most colorless, undemonstrative speech you can think of,
Bears, for good reason, find it embarrassing
Or at least disarming
And will forget their claws and cover their eyeteeth as an answer.
Meanwhile, move off, yielding the forest floor
As carefully as your honor.


# A GUIDE TO DUNGENESS SPIT

Out of wild roses down from the switching road between pools
We step to an arm of land washed from the sea.
On the windward shore
The combers come from the strait, from narrows and shoals
Far below sight. To leeward, floating on trees
In a blue cove, the cormorants
Stretch to a point above us, their wings held out like skysails.
Where shall we walk? First, put your prints to the sea,
Fill them, and pause there:
Seven miles to the lighthouse, curved yellow-and-grey miles
Tossed among kelp, abandoned with bleaching rooftrees,
Past reaches and currents;
And we must go afoot at a time when the tide is heeling.
Those whistling overhead are Canada geese;
Some on the waves are loons,
And more on the sand are pipers. There, Bonaparte's gulls
Settle a single perch. Those are sponges.
Those are the ends of bones.
If we cross the inner shore, the grebes and goldeneyes
Rear themselves and plunge through the still surface,
Fishing below the dunes
And rising alarmed, higher than waves. Those are cockleshells.
And these are the dead. I said we would come to these.
Stoop to the stones.
Overturn one: the grey-and-white, inch-long crabs come pulsing
And clambering from their hollows, tiptoeing sideways.

They lift their pincers
To defend the dark. Let us step this way. Follow me closely
Past snowy plovers bustling among sand-fleas.
The air grows dense.
You must decide now whether we shall walk for miles and miles
And whether all birds are the young of other creatures
Or their own young ones,
Or simply their old selves because they die. One falls,
And the others touch him webfoot or with claws,
Treading him for the ocean.
This is called sanctuary. Those are feathers and scales.
We both go into mist, and it hooks behind us.
Those are foghorns.
Wait, and the bird on the high root is a snowy owl
Facing the sea. Its flashing yellow eyes
Turn past us and return;
And turning from the calm shore to the breakers, utterly still,
They lead us by the bay and through the shallows,
Buoy us into the wind.
Those are tears. Those are called houses, and those are people.
Here is a stairway past the whites of our eyes.
All our distance
Has ended in the light. We climb to the light in spirals,
And look, between us we have come all the way,
And it never ends
In the ocean, the spit and image of our guided travels.
Those are called ships. We are called lovers.
There lie the mountains.

# Robert Penn Warren

∎

## MASTS AT DAWN

Past second cock-crow yacht masts in the harbor go slowly white.

No light in the east yet, but the stars show a certain fatigue.
They withdraw into a new distance, have discovered our
                                        unworthiness. It is long since

The owl, in the dark eucalyptus, dire and melodious, last called, and

Long since the moon sank and the English
Finished fornicating in their ketches. In the evening
                                        there was a strong swell.

Red died the sun, but at dark wind rose easterly, white
                        sea nagged the black harbor headland.

When there is a strong swell, you may, if you surrender to it, experience
A sense, in the act, of mystic unity with that rhythm. Your peace
                                        is the sea's will.

But now no motion, the bay-face is glossy in darkness, like

An old window pane flat on black ground by the wall, near
                                        the ash heap. It neither
Receives nor gives light. Now is the hour when the sea

Sinks into meditation. It doubts its own mission. The drowned cat
That on the evening swell had kept nudging the piles of the pier
                                        and had seemed

To want to climb out and lick itself dry, now floats free. On that
                        surface a slight convexity only, it is like

An eyelid, in darkness, closed. You must learn to accept the
                                        kiss of fate, for

The masts go white slow, as light, like dew, from darkness
Condenses on them, on oiled wood, on metal. Dew whitens in darkness.

I lie in my bed and think how, in darkness, the masts go white.

The sound of the engine of the first fishing dory dies seaward. Soon
In the inland glen wakes the dawn-dove. We must try

To love so well the world that we may believe, in the end, in God.

# Bruce Weigl

∎

## SNOWY EGRET

My neighbor's boy has lifted his father's shotgun and stolen
Down to the backwaters of the Elizabeth
And in the moon he's blasted a snowy egret
From the shallows it stalked for small fish.

Midnight. My wife wakes me. He's in the backyard
With a shovel so I go down half-drunk with pills
That let me sleep to see what I can see and if it's safe.
The boy doesn't hear me come across the dewy grass.
He says through tears he has to bury it,
He says his father will kill him
And he digs until the hole is deep enough and gathers
The egret carefully into his arms
As if not to harm the blood-splattered wings
Gleaming in the flashlight beam.

His man's muscled shoulders
Shake with the weight of what he can't set right no matter what,
But one last time he tries to stay a child, sobbing
Please don't tell. . . .
He says he only meant to flush it from the shadows,
He only meant to watch it fly
But the shot spread too far
Ripping into the white wings
Spanned awkwardly for a moment
Until it glided into brackish death.

I want to grab his shoulders,
Shake the lies loose from his lips but he hurts enough,
He burns with shame for what he's done,
With fear for his hard fathers's
Fists I've seen crash down on him for so much less.
I don't know what to do but hold him.
If I let go he'll fly to pieces before me.
What a time we share, that can make a good boy steal away,
Wiping out from the blue face of the pond
What he hadn't even known he loved, blasting
Such beauty into nothing.

# *Dara Wier*

∎

## THE GIFT

I had been thinking of Marcel Duchamp
    and the book he gave his sister.
He'd tied Euclidean geometry

    to a string to let
the four seasons and all the time
    of day and night

work it over, test it,
    offer it back to the birds
or whatever in nature would have it.

    It was his idea
to bring ideas down to earth again.
    I had been thinking

of the birth of our baby
    as she slept through the afternoon
in the solid quiet after a thunderstorm.

    I looked up
at the quiver of flowers
    in the middle of the table

and thought at first it must be me
    shaking from cold
or shaking with fears

    I wish her never tested.
Then I heard the Southern Crescent
    rattling north two blocks away

and thought of my long ride on it
    through mid-Atlantic snow
into Southern sleet and rain

to put behind me my grandfather's death
    and saw the train was the reason
the flowers were shaking.

# Richard Wilbur

∎

## PRAISE IN SUMMER

Obscurely yet most surely called to praise,
As sometimes summer calls us all, I said
The hills are heavens full of branching ways
Where star-nosed moles fly overhead the dead;
I said the trees are mines in air, I said
See how the sparrow burrows in the sky!
And then I wondered why this mad *instead*
Perverts our praise to uncreation, why
Such savor's in this wrenching things awry.
Does sense so stale that it must needs derange
The world to know it? To a praiseful eye
Should it not be enough of fresh and strange
That trees grow green, and moles can course in clay,
And sparrows sweep the ceiling of our day?

## THE LILACS

Those laden lilacs
                    at the lawn's end
Came stark, spindly,
                    and in staggered file,
Like walking wounded
                    from the dead of winter.
We watched them waken
                    in the brusque weather
To rot and rootbreak,
                    to ripped branches,
And saw them shiver
                    as the memory swept them
Of night and numbness
                    and the taste of nothing.
Out of present pain
                    and from past terror
Their bullet-shaped buds
                    came quick and bursting,
As if they aimed
                    to open with us!
But the sun suddenly
                    settled about them,
And green and grateful
                    the lilacs grew,

161

Healed in that hush,
                     that hospital quiet.
These lacquered leaves
                     where the light paddles
And the big blooms
                     buzzing among them
Have kept their counsel,
                     conveying nothing
Of their mortal message,
                     unless one should measure
The depth and dumbness
                     of death's kingdom
By the pure power
                     of this perfume.

# Nancy Willard

## CANNA LILY

Pushed out of the earth
like a note in a bottle,

it glistens with joy. A clump
of dirt clasps it still,
the broken seal of

the dead; this green scroll
from some dead sea
flowering.

## MUSHROOM

The army retreated and left
under the springs of Queen
Anne's lace and the skin
of cinquefoil, these

tender helmets: *earth star,*
*cloud's ear, chanterelle,*
mushrooms hunched and hid
like a covey of quail.

The gemmed puffball, gloved
in white kid, darkens
with age like the moon.
"Midwife to the fern and

the great oak, we bear no
flowers, stay nowhere long.
The wind seeds us, shakes
the wheeled loom of our

birth. Haloed in spores,
we lay at your feet our
elf-saddles and friendly
trumpets, unmusical but deep,

having the taste of time sealed
in amphoras and organ pipes:
in the eggs of mythical birds,
the taste of sleep."

# WHEN THERE WERE TREES

I can remember when there were trees,
great tribes of spruces who deckled themselves in light,
beeches buckled in pewter, meeting like Quakers,
the golden birch, all cutwork satin,
courtesan of the mountains; the paper birch
trying all summer to take off its clothes
like the swaddlings of the newborn.

The hands of a sassafras blessed me.
I saw maples fanning the fire in their stars,
heard the coins of the aspens rattling like teeth,
saw cherry trees spraying fountains of light,
smelled the wine my heel pressed from ripe apples,
saw a thousand planets bobbing like bells
on the sleeve of the sycamore, chestnut, and lime.

The ancients knew that a tree is worthy of worship.
A few wise men from their tribes broke through the sky,
climbing past worlds to come and the rising moon
on the patient body of the tree of life,
and brought back the souls of the newly slain,
no bigger than apples, and dressed the tree
as one of themselves and danced.

Even the conquerors of this country
lifted their eyes and found the trees
more comely than gold: *Bright green trees,*
*the whole land so green it is pleasure to look on it,*
*and the greatest wonder to see the diversity.*
*During that time, I walked among trees,*
*the most beautiful things I had ever seen.* *

Watching the shadows of trees, I made peace with mine.
Their forked darkness gave motion to morning light.
Every night the world fell to the shadows,
and every morning came home, the dogwood floating
its petals like moons on a river of air,
the oak kneeling in wood sorrel and fern,
the willow washing its hair in the stream.

And I saw how the logs from the mill floated
downstream, saw otters and turtles that rode them,
and though I heard the saws whine in the woods

---

\* *Adapted from the journals of Christopher Columbus,*
*as rendered in William Carlos Williams'* In the American Grain.

I never thought men were stronger than trees.
I never thought those tribes would join their brothers
the buffalo and the whale, the leopard, the seal, the wolf,
and the men of this country who knew how to sing them.

Nothing I ever saw washed off the sins of the world
so well as the first snow dropping on trees.
We shoveled the pond clear and skated under their branches,
our voices muffled in their huge silence.
The trees were always listening to something else.
They didn't hear the beetle with the hollow tooth
grubbing for riches, gnawing for empires, for gold.

Already the trees are a myth,
half gods, half giants in whom nobody believes.
But I am the oldest woman on earth,
and I can remember when there were trees.

# John Woods

■

## COMING TO THE SALT LICK

They will have it.
But not in the fodder
blowing ropily green
from their yellow mouths.

Now they are coming down from the pasture,
the swinging bell, the milky blaze,
heavy, imprecise, to the acrid stone.

Why do they want it?
Why do we need it?

It is our blood, remembering its own taste,
and when we took different paths
in the forest.

# Charles Wright

∎

## ARS POETICA

I like it back here

Under the green swatch of the pepper tree and the aloe vera.
I like it because the wind strips down the leaves without a word.
I like it because the wind repeats itself,
                         and the leaves do.

I like it because I'm better here than I am there,

Surrounded by fetishes and figures of speech:
Dog's tooth and whale's tooth, my father's shoe, the dead weight
Of winter, the inarticulation of joy . . .

The spirits are everywhere.

And once I have them called down from the sky, and spinning and
       dancing in the palm of my hand,
What will it satisfy?
                  I'll still have

The voices rising out of the ground,
The fallen star my blood feeds,
                     this business I waste my heart on.

And nothing stops that.


## AUTUMN

November the 1st. Gold leaves
Whisper their sentences through the blue chains of the wind.
I open a saint-john's-bread.

Green apples, a stained quilt,
The black clock of the heavens reset in the future tense.
Salvation's a simple thing.

# ABOUT THE EDITOR

Christopher Merrill is the author of two collections of poetry, *Workbook* and *Fevers & Tides;* co-translator (with Jeanie Puleston Fleming) of *Constellations* by André Breton and *Slow Down Construction* by Breton, René Char, and Paul Éluard; and editor of *Outcroppings: John McPhee in the West.* His poetry, fiction, essays, and reviews appear in a number of publications, including *Mississippi Review, The Paris Review, New Virginia Review,* and *The Pushcart Prize: Best of the Small Presses.* Editor of the Peregrine Smith Poetry Series, he directs the Santa Fe Writers' Conference and the Taos Conference on Writing and the Natural World. He lives with his wife Lisa, a violinist, in Santa Fe, New Mexico.

171

Reg Saner, "Waiting Out Rain, Sheltered by Overhang." Copyright © 1988 by Reg Saner. Reprinted by permission of the author. "Waiting Out Rain, Sheltered by Overhang" was first published in *Field*.

Richard Shelton, "Sonora for Sale." From *Selected Poems* by Richard Shelton, published by the University of Pittsburgh Press. Copyright © 1982 by Richard Shelton. Reprinted by permission of the author. "Glen Canyon on the Colorado." Copyright © 1991 by Richard Shelton. Reprinted by permission of the author. "Sonora for Sale." was first published in *The New Yorker*.

Charles Simic, "Strictly Bucolic" and "A Landscape with Crutches." From *Selected Poems 1963–1983* by Charles Simic. Copyright © 1985 by Charles Simic. Reprinted by permission of George Braziller, Inc.

Maurya Simon, "The Sadness of Rivers" and "Atomic Psalm." From *Days of Awe* by Maurya Simon, published by Copper Canyon Press. Reprinted by permission of the author. "*From* Spellbound: An Alphabet" from *Speaking in Tongues* by Maurya Simon. Copyright © 1990 by Maurya Simon. Reprinted by permission of Gibbs Smith, Publisher. "The Sadness of Rivers" was first published in *Poetry*.

Dave Smith, "Leafless Trees, Chickahominy Swamp." From *The Roundhouse Voices: Selected and New Poems* by Dave Smith. Copyright © 1985 by Dave Smith. Reprinted by permission of Harper & Row, Publishers, Inc.

Gary Snyder, "Piute Creek." From *Riprap* by Gary Snyder, published by Grey Fox Press. Copyright © 1958, 1959, 1965 by Gary Snyder. Reprinted by permission of the author. "The Real Work" from *Turtle Island* by Gary Snyder. Copyright © 1974 by Gary Snyder. Reprinted by permission of New Directions Publishing Company. "For All" from *Axe Handles* by Gary Snyder, published by North Point Press. Copyright © 1983 by Gary Snyder. Reprinted by permission of the author.

Marcia Southwick, "The Marsh." From *The Night Won't Save Anyone,* by Marcia Southwick, published by University of Georgia Press. Copyright © 1980 by Marcia Southwick. Reprinted by permission of the author.

William Stafford, "Ceremony," "In Response to a Question," "B.C." and "Fall Wind." From *Stories That Could Be True: New and Collected Poems* by William Stafford. Copyright © 1977 by William Stafford. Reprinted by permission of Harper & Row, Publishers, Inc.

Ruth Stone, "Snow Trivia" and "Laguna Beach." From *Second–Hand Coat, Poems New and Selected* by Ruth Stone, published by David R. Godine, Publisher. Copyright © 1987 by Ruth Stone. Reprinted by permission of the author.

Arthur Sze, "Parallax." From *River River* by Arthur Sze, published by Lost Roads Publishers. Copyright © 1987 by Arthur Sze. Reprinted by permission of the author.

Nathaniel Tarn, "*From* Journal of the Laguna de San Ignacio." From *At the Western Gates* by Nathaniel Tarn, published by Tooth of Time Books. Copyright © 1979, 1980, 1981, 1982, 1985 by Nathaniel Tarn. Reprinted by permission of the author.

Alberta Turner, "Small Animal." From *Need* by Alberta Turner. Copyright © 1971 by Alberta Turner. Reprinted by permission of Ashland Poetry Press.

Lee Upton, "Water Gardening." Copyright © 1988 by Lee Upton. Reprinted by permission of the author. "Water Gardening" was first published in *Field*.

Ellen Bryant Voigt, "The Bat." From *The Forces of Plenty* by Ellen Bryant Voigt. Copyright © 1983 by Ellen Bryant Voigt. Reprinted by permission of W. W. Norton & Company, Inc. "The Bat" was first published in *The New Yorker*.

David Wagoner, "Lost," "Meeting a Bear," and "A Guide to Dungeness Spit." From *Collected Poems, 1956–1976* by David Wagoner, published by Indiana University Press. Copyright © 1976 by David Wagoner. Reprinted by permission of the author.

Robert Penn Warren, "Masts at Dawn." From *Selected Poems 1923–1975* by Robert Penn Warren. Copyright © 1972 by Robert Penn Warren. Reprinted by permission of Random House, Inc.